Published by:

Tom Butler

baliyorahanu@gmail.com

Front cover artwork by:

Mary Butler

GHOST STORIES AND OTHER ISLAND TALES

CONTENTS

FOREWORD

After my father died in 2013, my mother found in his files the manuscript for a book that he had written about his days, more than fifty years earlier, as a colonial officer in the Gilbert and Ellice Islands. He had kept its existence a secret from his family, and had it typed up "on the quiet" some time in the early 2000s. It was clear from his notes that he had disguised some of the names of those who figure in the text. The book was a revelation to us, containing as it did details of a period in his life about which he hardly ever spoke.

After digitising the manuscript, I have edited it for flow and consistency, but with minimal changes to content. While it is clearly a memoir, this book also provides glimpses into a way of life – and an empire – that is now long vanished, and so I hope that it will be of interest to more than just my father's close family. It is in parts hilarious, in parts poetic, and there are also hints of frustration at the way the colonies were run from London, by a government that had more pressing matters to deal with than managing the remnants of a far-flung empire.

Tom Butler

Washington D.C.

July 2014

1

PREFACE – BIRMINGHAM

Charlie was a storeman with whom I worked. He was a stocky man with curly ginger hair and bright blue eyes in a rather leathery face which in the Midlands sun of Birmingham never lost its suety pallor. For the job he did a khaki coat would have been sensible, but he chose to wear white with heavy black boots buffed at least twice a day to a shine that equalled any advertisement for polish.

Charlie's domain was a shed where a stock of large ironmongery was kept, together with the specialised spares of the factory's machinery. Banks of small drawers held many lengths, threads and thicknesses of nuts, bolts, screws, nails, shims and washers, some of dull iron, others of shiny stainless steel, the frosted silver of aluminium or the red of copper. In open ended lockers were piles of chain, packs of hacksaw blades, sisal and wire rope and lengths of copper, iron and lead pipe. Locked up as they were "fingerable", were tools, screw drivers, hammers, pliers, drills, cold chisels, files and, wrapped up in wax paper, oiled ball-races, greased bearings and valves and nuts, bolts, screws and specialised fittings made for particular machines. Electric wire and cable, thick and thin, hung in labelled coils on long wooden poles.

In the care and availability of his supplies Charlie took a great pride. Should a break-down occur anywhere in the factory or an office, be it a broken bearing in a machine, a crossed thread in a typist's chair or a leaking ball valve in a lavatory cistern Charlie would have felt himself disgraced if he had not had the right spare for an instant repair to be started.

His stock cards, on which he recorded goings out and comings in, were meticulously kept and no verdigris or rust was ever permitted to soil any of his charges.

However, he had favourites and these were the largest, heaviest, most expensive and most important items of all his stock. Laid out with expanses of concrete to themselves, reverentially cushioned on wood in an attitude and atmosphere calling to mind a funeral parlour were the cylinders and coupling shafts of the rolling mills for which the factory existed, prone bodies of cold steel that could lie still for years, their surfaces painted protectively and their bearings and joints covered with clear brown grease. Designations were printed on cards "Coupling shaft for Loewe 3 high cold mill - male" and in proximity "Coupling shaft for Davy United 4 high hot mill - female". Charlie would walk once a week solemnly up and down the rows in which they were laid, as if he were in the aisle of a church, examining the bodies making sure their shrouds of paint had no chips or cracks and taking in for re-writing a card that became spotted or stained. Should an engineer come with a crane and a party of workmen to resurrect a corpse and carry it off to a mill to start its working life, Charlie would stand with his hands clasped and face beaming as a parson who has performed a wedding observes the bride and groom leaving his church. Now and again he would go to the mills and inspect his old parishioners making sure they were performing their duties and were well tended.

In the corner of his ever cold shed he had an office, warmed by a perpetually boiling kettle. As he was a lowly member of the factory hierarchy, it was some years since the office had been painted and the chairs were threadbare with their stuffing falling out. Here, after I had done my paper work or had had the uses of the various male and female bodies explained, we drank tea, over-sweetened with condensed milk, and gossiped.

Charlie talked of the Birmingham of his youth, the football teams and gangs to which he had belonged. By modern standards his groups of boys were tame, neither taking drugs - apart from alcohol - nor using knives or weapons, in their fights. They had sweethearts, drank beer and enjoyed boxing. The worst they did was shout impolite names at their rivals. This was not something Charlie talked about directly, but a verdict I had worked out. For Charlie, after a few preliminary mutterings, spoke in terms of dissolution and dissipation and how wicked he had been, before getting out of his chair, skipping around with eyes blazing and repeating endlessly that he had been saved. Details of real dissolution and dissipation would have been of much interest to me but were never forthcoming and it would have been too embarrassing to ask.

One sodden winter's day when the clouds dropped their drizzle from low over the high chimneys, I had to go to the shed where the mills were sheltered. The factory site was enormous and it was a depressing walk between dirty grey and brown buildings, circumnavigating the puddles, but with feet getting damper and damper. I passed the open doors of the shop where titanium was being welded under argon gas, with brilliant blue flashes flickering out and lighting up the road, and crossed over the rusting railway lines with old coal-fired engines puffing smoke and soot to the clouds. Noises of machines battering and contorting metal and the scream of cutting saws accompanied my voyage until I came to a shed 200 yards long and entered through a tin door which always jammed and needed a kick. Engulfed by incense and light, I was then in what I always called to myself "The Great Temple of Witon".

For the incense there was a mist of sweet, lubricating oil; for the light, the glare from arc lamps mounted in the ceiling and burning as blue and brilliant as the flashes of the titanium welders; for the gods, stout square-shouldered idols with wide shining mouths that devoured metal. In a straight line they were seated all the way to the far end of the building with a path of rollers running from one to another. With a clunk the first god gulped a bar of orange hot copper, squeezed it between cylinders and excreted it longer, thinner and wider to the rollers. The second god took in his coprophagous repast and delivered it yet thinner and dulling in hue towards the third, from which, slimmer and like a long tape of toffee, it was passed on. Blue enamelled, the deities were addressed as the "four high hot mills." "Four high" as each pair of cylinders had two backing cylinders pushing on them, preventing bowing and so ensuring that the copper was pressed to a uniform thickness. Beyond the line of "four highs" were "three highs", lesser divines devouring a lighter diet, which from one direction took in sheets between middle and lower cylinders, squeezed them, raised them and passed them back in the direction from which they had come between the middle and upper cylinders. Travelling at 4 miles per hour along the rollers, mill to mill, gaining in value, the copper emerged as "strip" and under this name was sold to the myriad workshops of Birmingham and the Midlands to be pressed, braised, rolled and sharpened into utensils for industry or goods for shops.

I was used to the mills and no longer saw them as impressive. Rather they were makers of money. As such they were given their elevated status and received their adulation. Attendant acolytes made sure the supply of copper was at the right temperature and entered the smiling maws square. Eyes were kept on the lubricating liquid which flowed over the cylinders. Meters indicated the use of electricity - neither too little nor too much, and no flickering of needles, all indicators of indisposition. Bearings were anointed with oil and grease and weekly examinations made for crackings and pittings. Engineers, acolytes of a higher status, were on call to listen for untoward internal mutterings and to carry out fitness tests.

At the periphery of the factory site, far removed from the molochs and their smoke and noise, accountants crouched over books and dematerialised the outflow of metals into sets of figures and statistics which they compared against other sets of figures and statistics showing costs of production, maintenance and overheads. They were heartless men, who it seemed to me would have scorned (as an anathema) Wordsworth's lines "High heaven rejects the lore of nicely calculated less or more" and who were unmoved by the mercilessness of the gods when they took a life or inflicted an injury seemingly on a whim. For them, all human damage could be converted to and measured in ciphers, and in my imagination they resembled Aztec priests to whom the letting of blood and sacrifice of life was necessary for the continued existence and good of the community. An alert worker attempted to arrest a wayward bolt from consumption and had his forearm pulped in the rollers. A custodian of an acid bath was scalded and lost an eye. The medical costs and disability payments were recorded and debited to the gods' accounts with figures hidden in columns equating to pain, mutilation and disability.

Our attendants to the local gods served a higher and more powerful order of divinity. The members of this order were invisible but their existence was exhibited by brass plates on mills' flanks bearing names of an indeterminate internationalism - Davy United, Loewe - and of comfortable towns which the attendants envied but might never visit - Bournemouth, Bristol, Zurich - far removed from the grime of Birmingham. There, subtle theologians sifted figures for suppliers' prices, spot and forward, watched rates of interest, absorbed the factory's running and overhead costs and made projections of sales and market expectations.

When they had done their sums, they costed and designed our gods and tried to convince the capitalist kings in London that figures would grow into greater figures and add to the profits and dividends exhibited in a shiny company report.

Unseen and unknown in person the members of the highest order of divinity might be, but their distant if urbane displeasure was far more feared in our factory than anything an idol could do to a human. Greater damage was done to a balance sheet by a still and silent machine than by a mutilated and screaming man. Idols had to turn and squeeze without remit, day in, day out. Only for half an hour in the middle of the day were the workers allowed to break. On one wet and gloomy day this they were doing as I entered the shed. The workers were walking to the end of the building where the first mill of the manufacturing line stood. Next to the mill was a furnace where the copper was heated and men found the warmth made a pleasant place in which to eat their sandwiches. In the crowd of grimy blue-overalled bodies, somebody in a white coat stood out. He was carrying a chair and when he turned his head I recognised Charlie. Putting the chair down by the mill he stood on it and wrote in chalk on the side of the machine. His words were:

"The foxes have holes and the birds of the air have nests; but the Son of Man hath not where to lay His Head".

He turned round, nodded at me and started to preach. The congregation was not very attentive but they at least kept silence. Since I, as it were, was in the front pew I tried to look interested. Mention of dissipation brought me to life but when no details were provided a gloom as dull as the day overcame me. "Foxes" reminded me immediately of Dorset and one of the few foxes I had ever seen when sitting in a field and watching the sea over a hedge. There was green grass, blue water and a warm sun. But in this city of grime and ugliness nature was first subdued and then lied to by man. Were names more false ever given to a railway station than "Snow Hill" or to the sooty grass and brick of Bourneville than "garden village"? My lodgings were in Handsworth Wood Road although when I had bicycled along the road all I had come to was a coal mine - and even that was a disappointment. In an era of nationalisation and left wing government the flag flown over the mine was neither deepest red nor even cherry red but a respectable mediocre blue. The men in my lodgings lived in their own worlds, some real but dull - like the one whose main problem in life was to work out a process for anodising aluminium white - others unreal but colourful - an English teacher for whom only Victorian literature existed, and a bank clerk whose favourite reading was the social news in the yellow press - parties, scandal and money of the titled or rich.

The factory, Birmingham and the country around I all hated and the words of Hillaire Belloc gave me comfort that somebody else, a poet, felt as I did;

"I am living in the Midlands

That are sodden and unkind

The great hills of the South Country

Come back into my mind"

and Charlie, having dealt with the comforts religion brought him, paused and then slowly, with great significance and almost shouting the words: "Our soul is escaped even as bird out of the snare of the fowler."

I thought 'Charlie, I disagree with you but you have a vision. There is more to life than a succession of more comfortable offices, bigger houses in more

6

prestigious suburbs, four or five extra days holiday a year and bigger and more expensive cars all in a town that I do not like and surrounded by countryside that I do not like and, at the end, a retirement which the company's actuarial figures showed you would last six months'.

'What shall I do?' I pondered but not for long, having just read a book about them; 'I shall join the Colonial Service and go to the Gilbert and Ellice Islands. That will be fun and also worthwhile'.

1.   IMPERIAL TRAINING

Birmingham pushed me out but childhood memories, on which perhaps I had been dwelling too much, pulled me away from Britain. My father had been an engineer and soldier in India. It was in India that he had met and married my mother and it was in India that my brother and I had been born. I was four when we left to live in England, and my memories are scant although varied and vivid. Our bungalow was on the banks of the Brahmaputra, flowing broad and brown out of the Himalayas to join, I remember being told, the Ganges. Once I escaped my ayah and walked by myself along the side of it. This brought a great scolding upon my ayah and me. The river had crocodiles in it, both gharials, long snouted fish eaters, and muggers, broad snouted flesh and everything-that-goes eaters. If I ever did such a thing again I would surely be devoured. This came dramatically from my father who was a keen fisherman and caught enormous fish in the river called mahseer - one so big that it stuck out of both doors in the back of his car - a car which, when he went "on tour" seemed to spend most of its time being pushed by an elephant out of the mud in which it was stuck. My mother, however, could add little directly to the scolding. Hindustani was my first language and I always had to ask my ayah for a translation of anything my mother said. It took three weeks on the boat back to England to lose the language and become fluent in English.

I was also caught one day taking too much interest in a krait, a small but very poisonous snake, light brown with coloured bands round its body. It was nervously wriggling along a semi-circular drain that was too deep to get out and I can see myself well clear of it - the evil of snakes had been a source of much exhortation - wondering what it was going to do. It was I suppose beaten to a pulp but I only remember being told it was more dangerous than a cobra, as it was often unnoticed and, being thin, was better able to turn round and bite a hand or foot placed mistakenly on its body. Our province, Assam, was "jungly" and the forests full - of tigers, leopards and pythons - even fuller by far than they were in the talk of our town-bred servants and Europeans.

The servants - some 20 to 30 - were my friends, particularly the gardeners, and particularly one gardener. We often went up to Shilong, a hill station. On a steep hill, where jungle came down to a narrow road where only one-way traffic was allowed, I suddenly noticed my "mahli" squatting on the running board behind the battery. I demanded that he be let into the car but was told that "he was used to that" and would not come to any harm. He didn't, but I can't recall what he held on to. Also among my friends was a monkey - hooluk in Hindustani. He was small with thin black hair and long arms. We used to walk round the garden holding hands.

Apart from my memories of India my parents fed me for years with their recollections, and when they got together with other retired Anglo-Indians I would listen to their stories. There were seventy statutory public holidays a year in India so there was plenty of time for people to play sport and enjoy themselves. My father also related his adventures in "Mespot" (modern day Iraq) during the first world war where he was fighting the Turks and also the Kurds (in rebellion), two shillings and sixpence for a plateful of caviar, a climate where the temperature would be over 120 in the day and so cold at night that paraffin froze and tents were pitched in holes dug in the ground. An Indian officer in his regiment borrowed his shot gun and, putting the end of the barrel under water, shot a fish. The barrel split open, the gun was useless and "he never replaced it".

Two of my father's brothers were "out East", one in southern India and the other in Indonesia, (then the Dutch East Indies), Brunei and Malaya. Two of his sisters knew the east going "out" from time to time to run houses for bachelor brothers. "Teddy was very down one day so he went to the market and came back with a bear cub. Of course it was a perfect nuisance." The same aunt chaperoned Teddy's wife on a boat to Singapore for her marriage and then went to stay with the newly marrieds in the Caramoan Islands. She was the only woman allowed into the local club - a piece of snobbery of which she thoroughly disapproved - and nearly got engaged (I surmise) to a much older reprobate doctor who gave her some beautiful jade. My mother had a brother in India and also this side of my family had friends in their retirement who talked lovingly of the pink parts of the globe.

In 1934 we left India to live in Surrey. To reach the unknown land of "home" we travelled by train to Calcutta and then across India to Bombay. Such a journey now would be exciting but my only two recollections are of watching an Indian goatherd driving his flock across a bridge that was retracting into a quay in the Calcutta docks and wondering whether he would fall into the water and of a bulge in the side of our compartment, grubby railway-brown like the rest of the train and of no seeming use or purpose. I asked my father and he told me it held a block of ice, 80 lbs I think, to keep us cool over night. What I do not remember, but wish I could and can reconstruct vividly from what my mother told me and with the help of adult imagination, is turning on a hydrant - bright red - on the deck - spotless white - of our ship when we boarded. Excited Italians (we were travelling Lloyd Trestino) discovered it and rushed to turn off the flood that had been created and there was much criticism from other boarding passengers of the ship's captain for allowing the decks to be washed at such a time. He never found he was the verbal whipping boy for the perpetrator who, hustled by his mother, had disappeared.

I have a memory of Venice, where we landed, which is real and much more of a favourite. I am lying in a gondola under a pale evening sky on a narrow canal between high walls. A man is above and is working a long oar and we are travelling silently and comfortably on dark water.

Duly we arrived in London - excising that great dislike of ocean travellers, the Bay of Biscay, by taking a train. Of this I have no memory although if I had it would surely have been refreshed as thirty years later I again travelled, on leave from Africa, to Venice by Lloyd Trestino, with a wife in place of my mother, and two children, took a gondola along a canal and a train to Paris, no stop-over, and on to London.

We were met at Victoria by the aunt (May) who had coped with her brother, Teddy, in Malaya and chaperoned his betrothed on the voyage to her wedding. When I was a teenager and later, she became very much a favourite, having experienced, done and seen things of much interest: from being booed at by a horrible small red headed boy at her dancing class (Winston Churchill); when at school in Dresden, "which had a king", being taken to the railway station to see Bismarck (face like a blood hound); in 1911, from the streets seeing the Tsar in Berlin among other visiting monarchs. "When he passed the soldiers lining the road turned around, faced the spectators and pointed their bayonets at us." (Many Germans she met, particularly the army officer husbands of school friends told her "England is finished.") In 1923 she was in Rome at the time of the first anniversary of Mussolini's march on that city and saw the Duce.

As the eldest of the family when her parents died young she brought up her younger brothers and sister, then worked in a mission in London and ran a Church Army hostel in Place Pigalle in Paris for the English dancing girls at the Folies Bergeres. "We had a fire in a chimney one day and I called the fire brigade. Not only did they have a peculiar way of putting out the fire with wet blankets (anything un-English was not approved of) but as soon as they

10

discovered where they were, they were a perfect nuisance". She spoke French and Italian in addition to her school German, acquired an A.R.C.M. (music teaching qualification), loved Rome above all cities and if she could not live in England that was where she would choose to be.

But that was all to come. A small composed elderly woman, she met us on a grey platform on a cold grey London day and watched while her brother and his family got out of the train. Huge grey fur buttons on her coat caught my eye and when I saw the whole coat was fur I realised we had come to a very different land to India and that life was to change. A mark of the change, and diametrically different to the sprawling bungalow in Assam, my parents bought a house, tight and neat in a semi-rural area and near a station with fast trains to "town".

Although when he gossiped with other Anglo-Indians in a glow of retrospection about the pleasures of life "out east," my father in a gloomier mood in his family spoke of having "sweated it out in India for twenty five years." Of the two sides of his life the romance of India definitely won for my brother and myself, and was encouraged by our mother. We had Kipling read to us and then read him for ourselves along with books of adventure and wild life in Scotland, where my mother had been born and bred, and of tropical jungles and life. Rhinoceroses, tigers, elephants and people armed with spears and bows proved much more interesting than foxes, wild cats and red deer, however many points they might have, and kilted highlanders living (I worked out) in the cold and damp. I went to school in Surrey, ran away from it when it evacuated to Dorset in 1940, enjoyed the war - we lived within the triangle of Battle of Britain aerodromes, Biggin Hill, Kenley, and Croydon. We saw dog fights and doodle bugs (V1s) and air raids on London at night, flares coming down, search lights beaming up, anti-aircraft shells exploding on high, shrapnel through the larder window and barrage balloons down the road. It was all very exciting for a boy, and I looked forward to joining up. When I did National Service after the war my posting was to Hong Kong where I travelled by troop ship, stopped at ports whose names I knew well from Egypt onwards, and was back in the east. Then to university and work in ICI's metals division. My father regarded my "bringing up" as finished and that I was successfully launched on a career and off his hands.

My family protested about my intentions to leave my "good job"- a "good job" I have always assumed being a polite way of saying a well paid job - and was told that the job "would get more interesting". They also pointed out that the empire was, as my father and an uncle said "being dis-established" and "going down the drain" so that I could be shortly without any job at all. Against this I said I would take a chance. Retrospectively I was wrong but then, if my factory's actuarial figures for the length of life on pension that I would have "enjoyed" after retirement were correct, I would have been dead long ago.

I passed an interview (no entrance exam) for an appointment in the government of the Gilbert and Ellice Islands Colony, shook the slush and mud of Snow Hill station off my shoes and departed to Cambridge for a year on a Colonial Service training course for cadet administrative officers.

The appointment was probationary and to secure it I had to pass the Cambridge course and its exams and then, in the Gilbert and Ellice Islands, law and language exams within three years of first appointment and, within five years, either "the first language on the higher grade or the second language on the lower grade". It seemed years of exams but of more concern a colonial mandarin of the highest, seemingly astronomical, importance had to be satisfied with my services and general conduct - otherwise it was out on an ear. This mandarin was not only His Excellency the Governor of Fiji but also Her Britannic Majesty's High Commissioner for the Western Pacific (also "Excellent"). He was responsible in this second capacity for the good governance of the British Solomon Islands Protectorate, the Anglo share of the Anglo-French Condominium of the New Hebrides and the Gilbert and Ellice Islands Colony which included the Phoenix Islands, where Canton Island was under joint British-American administration, and the Line Islands, where 2 of the islands, Starbuck and Malden, were under the "personal jurisdiction" of the High Commissioner. Pitcairn was I think also included in "HE's" far flung and watery domain. However, His Britannic Majesty's High Commissioner was at least a year away, the language exams even further away - and where would there be a problem? My father spoke and, right to left, wrote fluent Hindustani while my uncle in southern India, I had been told, spoke several Indian languages. So up to Cambridge I went with a light heart and a keen interest to find what colonial administration was all about.

There were some sixty colonial cadets in Cambridge and at the beginning of the first term we were summoned by our supervisor to a meeting in the Colonial Services Club. He sorted us out into bottle-washers (administrators), twenty plus, and farmers (agriculturalists), thirty plus, whom he handed over to an ex-Tanganyikan agricultural officer, whereupon they disappeared to a lecture theatre and out of our lives. The administrators had our names called and we were grouped into colonies. The biggest groups, five or six in each, were going to Northern Rhodesia and Nyasaland, two or three each to Uganda, Kenya and Tanganyika, one to West Africa, one to Aden, one to Southern Africa, one to Hong Kong and two to the western Pacific. I was one of the two assigned to the Western Pacific, the other was an Australian who had already served three years in the Solomon Islands and New Hebrides and was doing his course late.

To the supervisor we were all "chaps". He was a tall thin Irishman and worked hard refereeing inter-college rugby matches so was fit with a springy step. Officially he was of course selling the Empire and Commonwealth. "Nigeria (well on the way to independence) put in for eighty cadets this year and did not get one, there will be plenty of jobs for you chaps". Privately and after a beer or two he was rather otherwise.

"The Germans machine-gunned whole villages but the blacks preferred them to the British. They knew where they stood and never could understand our courts."

The men - no female colonial administrators ever existed as far as I know - spent most of their time learning African languages while the Hong Kongers learnt Mandarin, the Solomon Islander already knew pidgin (Melanesian style not West African] and I was given a Gilbertese grammar but nobody to help me with it nor, happily, to examine me.

We came from a number of universities in Britain, the most numerous single group being from Oxford. The Oxonians never settled to their year's life at Cambridge and were difficult to relate to. In my first encounter with them after the inaugural meeting at the Colonial Services Club when they were gossiping together I was asked: "Which are the OK colleges here?"

I could not give them an answer but listening to them sounding each other out gathered which were on the up or down at Oxford, the most desirable apparently being the one which had "a peer on every staircase" - a new and seemingly most laudable achievement for the college. At the end of our year, one of their number rather surprised me. He was at, I would judge, the best known of all Oxbridge colleges, but announced that if he had not been able to go to Oxford he would rather not have gone to any university at all. His companion agreed and they then fell to discussing dining when on tour, the ordering of "goodies" from Fortnums and the importance of drinking port after dinner. (Not the most suitable beverage in a tropical climate).

Much of the time when I should have been learning my language was spent trying to find out more about the Gilbert and Ellice Islands. This was

13

difficult. The libraries of Cambridge produced nothing and the lecturer in anthropology I shared with the Solomon Island cadet seemed to think they were rather dull. The Trobriand Islanders had sex lives of immense interest, on which he could talk for hours, as well as another South Seas people who, although active practitioners, knew nothing about the consequences of sexual intercourse but kept their women out of the sea as they believed immersion in the Pacific caused pregnancy. The tribes of Papua and New Guinea he thought might still hunt heads but the Gilbertese and Ellice as he put it "long had the stuffing knocked out of them" by missionaries and European Government - "the last cannibal in the Ellice Islands must have died at the turn of the century, but make sure you paddle your canoe on the correct side. If you don't you may be in trouble."

The reading provided by the Colonial Office was depressing. "Hints on the Preservation of Health in Tropical countries" described some frightening diseases - yaws, jiggers, blackwater fever, yellow fever, typhoid, Singapore foot, elephantiasis, leprosy, worms - hooked, round and flat, and dysentery - amoebic and bacillary.

One wondered how much time it would be possible to spend out of hospital. Other papers described salary scales with "efficiency bars" and "notches", pensions, entitlements, housing allowance, dress regulations and disciplinary procedures. Only one phrase in the officialese hinted at the romance of the South Seas. "For formal evening wear cummerbunds are worn. The colour of the cummerbund worn by officers of the Western Pacific High Commission is a pale blue reminiscent of surf breaking on a tropical reef.

Apart from being administrators we were all to be magistrates, ex—officio, in our Colonies with both criminal and civil powers. To train us in our legal duties law was the subject to which the second greatest amount of time was committed. At first this seemed simple with clear principles but, as we got into it, it became a hotch-potch with principle obscured by tradition, rules, over-rules, statutory law, case law and judicial guidance, "binding" and "obiter", from judges of differing importance.

If the law was novel and interesting Local Government was not, and to Local Government with its rates, services, councillors, mayors, town clerks and aldermen I took an instant dislike. Unfortunately it was considered important and, besides incredibly dull reading and lectures, we had to give up two weeks of the Lent Vacation to a secondment for practical experience of a local authority. An uncle and aunt of mine lived in Argyll and it seemed to me that the Colonial Office could help with the fare to see them. So I suggested my secondment to study local government could best be made in the Hebrides as remote islands with many problems similar to the Gilberts. My argument, sharpened I liked to think by newly acquired knowledge of the law, was accepted and by train and steamer I found myself dispatched to Stornoway.

Two weeks spent in Lewis and Harris were helpful in showing me all facets of local government from the functioning of the police - a remote constable had made one arrest in twenty five years - to the work of the hospital, crammed with T.B. patients looking pink and healthy. But most practically, hitch-hiking on a fishing boat to Campbeltown, how to deal with sea sickness - lie flat on your back and eat nothing but dry biscuits. As a law abiding Briton it was also a surprise that the inhabitants of these islands regarded people from the mainland of Scotland with suspicion and as unwelcome masters and people from England, particularly London, as members of a distant and hostile land. The Hebrideans were a close knit community with their own language and customs, many of them Roman Catholics in a country of Protestants, and with a sense of identity and a wish to preserve their own way of life. An attempt by MacFisheries between the wars to establish a wholesale fishing industry and better the life of the people had evidently failed because the locals had not been consulted and apparently did not wish to become workers in a large factory while, shortly before my visit, the whole of Stornoway had rallied to support the wife and family of a man who had assaulted the Fiscal (Magistrate). The man had - rightly - been convicted of drunkenness but when the Fiscal, a mainlander, took it on himself to upbraid him and the generality of the local community as being idle and feckless this was more than the prisoner could take. He waited outside the court and seriously battered the Fiscal when he left the building. Another mainland Fiscal had to be sent in who gave the man a year in gaol. This was when the heart of the community was touched and a whip around provided better for the wife and children than the husband and father had ever done. It was a lesson to take to heart.

We also had on the course lectures or talks from officers serving in the field in various colonies as well as a junior minister in the Colonial Office. A Provincial Commissioner from Kenya talked on the Mau-Mau as a terrorist and political organisation. Despite thousands of British troops, armed auxiliaries, the services of loyal blacks, road blocks, curfews and aerial searches the Mau-Mau had suffered their most serious reverse from the arms of two elderly women. They dined with revolvers next to their wine glasses.

15

When two Mau-Mau burst into the room shooting they shot back and killed them. So low were women held in the estimation of the Kikuyu people from which the Mau-Mau were recruited that the movement's morale was heavily dented and its members scorned.

The provincial commissioner impressed us, being business-like and knowledgeable with an air of authority. The junior minister of the Government was quite the opposite. He waffled about the empire maturing into a global commonwealth, culturally led by the theatre world of London, while his work seemed to be conducted through an extensive range of miscellaneous contacts out of his past. "At school with me", "at Oxford with me", "in my college", "in my regiment" and "the cox in my boat" - a Siamese prince with whom he had an exciting ride in "his Bentley" at night through Bangkok. What he achieved was not clear while he displayed all the evasiveness of a man of the House of Commons in giving crooked answers to inconvenient questions.

The most useful information on the type of life I was to lead came from the Australian who had done three years in the Western Pacific. He and his wife asked me to their flat for dinner and over a couple of beers - "not the best my beaut but I am getting used to it" he said."The Colonial Office doesn't know and the Colonial Office doesn't want to know. Its ministers are only put there because they might do damage in another ministry that could lose votes in an election. If little Tootsie doesn't get her cake for tea in England that's a political disaster. If half a million people don't have bread in Africa, that's normal. It would only worry the Colonial Office if the reds got in but then they don't know how the reds travel. That man who spoke to us the other night, Harrington-Jones, he met our Commissioner of Police when he was on leave over here and said to him 'Do you have much trouble controlling communists who come in by train?' We are in the British Solomon Islands Protectorate. They are islands, islands with sea round them and if he had ever looked at a map he would have seen there is no railway line in the Protectorate and no bridge of any sort to Indonesia or anywhere else. There is no show in London worse than the Colonial Office. What they do nobody knows. If you are going to do anything in this job it's up to you and you will do it despite the Colonial Office - it is war between them and us".

I digested this verbal battery given to one of the great offices of state responsible to Parliament and the Crown for the protection and good governance of millions of people in vast areas of land worldwide. From talking to ex-soldiers of the two world wars it sounded similar to the War

Office - so out of touch with reality that the Chief of Staff in France who went to the front line and saw the mud after the Battle of the Somme in 1916 sat down and wept saying "Good God, did we send men to fight in this?"

I said something about the High Commissioner for the Western Pacific.

"Not interested. He is governor of Fiji and that's bigger and more important than all of the rest of the Western Pacific put together. The Western Pacific is run by his A.D.C. from a shed in the garden of Government house in Suva. That's 1,400 miles from us and 1,500 miles from the Gilberts. Only one High Commissioner has ever been to us or to the Gilberts and that was Sir Harry Luke in the 1930s when he had a holiday cruise before retiring. You are on your own, mate, in the Solomons, the Gilberts or the New Hebrides and that can be fun, particularly in the New Hebrides. I was meant to go to the Solomons on first appointment but they had staff problems in the New Hebrides and I spent eight months in Vila - that's the capital. Well, as you know it's a Condominium, and to start the British won't approve anything the French propose and the French won't approve anything the British want to do. So all the administration is duplicated. There are two Resident Commissioners and for each District two District Officers and two police officers but for the Courts there are four in each District - a British Court, a French Court, a Joint Court and a Condominium Court. Well, here was I, a cadet, and when I arrived in Vila I was going to be a full blown District Officer on my own - no French, no law, no administrative experience. But as I got off the boat the customs officer said the British Resident Commissioner wanted to see me in an hour's time. So I changed and went up to the Residency and saw Morgan. He is a nice old chap but only interested in fishing. So we talked a bit and then he said 'I am afraid I have another job for you.' My face must have fallen for he said: 'No, you won't lose your District but we are a bit under-strength in my office here and I am appointing you Acting Assistant Resident Commissioner. It's mainly a formality.'

"So there was I, second in command of the British side of the condominium. 'Then, unfortunately, there is a second or, I suppose, a third job for you. The Commandant of Police has to go on sick leave. Poor chap's got an operation coming up in Melbourne so you will have to look after the police for a while. That's a bit more work as you will be the only white in the force but the French commandant will help you out. Nice office you have got there'. We chatted a bit about the jobs and he asked me up to dinner. 'My French opposite number will be there - decent chap although speaks very little

English.' He paused, and I got up. 'The Chief Justice would like to meet you. Good man and likes birds. Would you go over to his office? It is the other side of the compound and the messenger will show you the way.'"

"So I was taken over to meet the Chief Justice who was also very charming and after we had talked a bit he said 'We are rather short staffed at present. I am signing your appointment this morning as a magistrate but we have another job for you on the Joint Court.' So I asked what the Joint Court was and he explained that when British and French were involved in a case they had to go to the Joint Court for a settlement or prosecution. And I asked what the other courts were for. He said British courts were for the British and natives who are involved in British law, French courts for the French and natives involved in French law. Condominium court is for the natives if British, French and natives are involved. It sounds complicated but it works quite well. He got up to show me out when I remembered I did not know what I was to do in the Joint Court. 'Oh I didn't tell you, did I? You are to be the Judge. Only ad hoc of course but you will have full judicial powers. And would you mind calling in on the Attorney General - there is his office down the passage.'

"And he was also a charming fellow. He had won an M.C. as a paratrooper in the war and was interested in shooting but said the best sport he got was shooting flying fish. And when I left him he said he also had a job for me and that was as Public Prosecutor. 'You can look in once a week and I believe you are Commandant of Police?' I said yes I was, and a Judge. So he said 'Well, they will all go well together as long as you keep to different courts and don't get your files muddled. Let's go and have a beer.'

"Did you get paid for all those jobs?" I asked.

"No chance. Just the same as you will get, eleven hundred Australian pounds a year. Say eight hundred sterling."

"And worked all day and all night?"

"No. Not that either. Nothing goes on in the New Hebrides. Nothing. The Poms and Frogs don't hit it off and they won't agree to anything. That suits the planters and that suits the Abos - Melanesians. No interference as long as you don't commit a crime. I had to write letters to myself to keep the records clear, particularly District Officer to Assistant Resident Commissioner but then I would go up to the Resident's office twice a week and sort out problems with His Honour and write back to myself as District Officer. I had to do a bit of finukery on the judicial side. I took a confession from a thief

18

whom I had to prosecute in the condominium court. So I did my prosecuting, called on myself as a witness and took to the witness box and read the confession. Then I returned to prosecuting and asked questions. I also got my schedules a bit tight as Judge and took evidence from a witness over the telephone and shouted it out in Court. The Court record had to be carefully worded. Our law lecturer would not have liked it. Don't worry mate, the Gilberts are meant to be a bit more proper."

He ended the evening by asking why I wanted to go to the Gilbert Islands. I mumbled something in reply about Birmingham and worthwhile jobs.

"That's all right then but one of the last cadets to go there said it was because it was as far away as he could get from his mother-in-law. He didn't last long."

2. TEN NABETARI

One of the cadets at Cambridge failed all his exams. He was a thin reticent man whom we hardly ever saw and the general consensus was that the Aden Protectorate to whose deserts he was being consigned was a most suitable posting. The Colonial Office appeared unconcerned about his lack of academic success and with approximately what he wore, plus a canvas bath, cooking pots and a primus he was the first on a boat out of England. My friend Dugald, sandy haired, short and a violent Scots nationalist who had helped steal the Stone of Scone from Westminster Abbey departed with a newly acquired wife to Cape Town on the way to Nyasaland. Here the energy which he had determined to devote to liberating Africans from British rule was diverted by the frustrations of the Dark Continent into a ferocious nitpicking and love of regulation and order so that after he had got on the wrong side of everybody in his district he was transferred to the Treasury where in a distant room of his own he was a great success.

For my part, I departed by ship on the great imperial route to the Far East and Australia - Bay of Biscay, Gibraltar, Port Said, Suez Canal, Aden, Bombay, Colombo, Fremantle, Adelaide and Melbourne, first class and with 8 chances a day to eat - eagerly taken by most elderly women on board - although for me the greatest luxury was having an enormous bath in hot sea water every evening. A series of pleasures I have never been able to repeat.

In Melbourne I got off and reported to the agents of the Gilbert and Ellice Islands Colony Government. They were efficient and helpful and did all to ensure the necessities of life were provided for the first six months of colonial existence. I was booked into a starred hotel and soon learnt to approve of Australian breakfasts of steak and lamb's fry and to acquire a taste for Victoria Bitter.

The breakfasts were leisurely and the dining room was shared with wrinkly sheep farmers who consumed their vast amounts of meat at a calm and dignified pace. Not so the drinking. The public bar was filled from 5 o'clock with pale gabbling businessmen flooding their bellies with unbelievable rapidity and making a defensive circle of filled pint mugs round their place at the bar. The beer in the circle was for consumption when the bar stopped sales at 6 and before the drinkers were turned out at 7 to make for home.

After a week of leisure I was put on a boat steaming to Ocean Island to load phosphate.

For 10 days we travelled north thudding our way across endless water seeing no boat, no land and, except flying fish, no life. I was the only passenger and, after looking over the ship stem to stern and keel to mast, for three days I read two books a day. I then reduced the reading to one book a day, joined the ship's crew as an unpaid chipper of paint and pestered the ship's officers at mid-day when they took sights into showing me how navigation was done. Ocean Island[1] appeared one evening, a dark hump sitting on the water directly opposing our path. Little yellow dots glowed on its side and from one point at the base a light flashed. On the bridge the telegraph rang to the engine room "Slow". The engine room returned the call and the steady thumping that had become part of life since we left port slowed and hushed like a heart which no longer had to beat. I had arrived in colonial waters.

Setting foot on the Colony's land in the morning was more exciting and hazardous. A smart man in khaki and blue with a brown weathered face and a toothbrush moustache boarded and introduced himself as Hamish, the Officer Commanding, Gilbert and Ellice Islands Armed Constabulary. He then explained as Chief Immigration Officer he needed my passport and as Chief Customs Officer had to clear my baggage. With a minimum of words he finished his business and led me to a rectangular platform with stanchions and a chain sitting on deck. From the side of his mouth but looking me in the face he squeezed out "Hold tight" and stepping on the platform I grabbed the chain. A derrick wound in a wire and with a lurch and sway we were up, tipped at an angle and swinging away from the ship out to sea. We stopped, swung backwards and forwards and came almost to rest. Twenty feet away the ocean sloshed smartly against the side of the ship. Below, a little boat rose on slopes and slipped into troughs of dark blue Pacific that had taken on a sinister power quite alien to the carpet like smoothness to which for days past I had become accustomed.

"Get ready to jump" slid out of Hamish's mouth and suddenly the boat was coming up and we were going down. We met on a ridge, the platform bumped, the policeman said "Now", a brown man held up the chain and I jumped, slid and fell on to a seat. The policeman followed and as the

---

[1] Now known as Banaba Island

21

platform went away the boat's motor sped up and we heaved into a trough and up the following slope.

Thirty yards on, the motor spluttered. Sixty yards on, it stopped and we slowed to a halt. The brown man who had helped me on board gargled loudly and a second brown man appeared from the engine room dressed in khaki printed with the broad arrows of the Sydney family and holding a crank handle. He fitted it into the end of the engine and heaved it round. The engine refused resuscitation and the two Gilbertese conferred with the policeman before starting a dismantling operation.

The boat's motion was foul and I looked with longing towards the land. Above the cliffs there were green trees and a slanting road on which people walked. Houses stood under palms, boats moved in the harbour and near it stood a building, outside which flew a Union Jack. The District Office, I surmised, and as a future place of work, tried to look at it with interest, not very successfully.

The boat was drifting to the west and thinking that I should know something about the local currents I asked Hamish whether they changed in the direction from which they came. He hadn't spoken to me since telling me to jump but now he seemed to think the situation needed some explanation. He slanted his mouth up at one corner and I realised words were about to come but again he looked me full in the face. Grudgingly he spoke out of the slanted up corner. His lips moved very little and he seemed as if he were a ventriloquist trying to make his voice come a foot or two away to the side. His accent was New Zealand. "You are very lucky to be seeing the island from here. As for the current about which you asked. No, the current doesn't change. Always from the east at one to two knots".

The slanted-up corner lost some of its tilt and the policeman's words came from closer to his face. This way of speaking I thought must have come from years of experience in court, designed to keep an eye on the prisoner in the dock but putting words clearly to the magistrate on the bench.

"You are right, my boy, but we haven't had a decent blow for 4 years. So it does not happen very often. If you are going to be sick do it over the side". I did - ex bacon and eggs. If I had known it was the last bacon I was going to have for 2 years I would have been perhaps sad as well as sick. As it was I felt better.

"Sorry."

"Alright, don't feel so good myself."

Hamish spoke to the Gilbertese crew, almost now in the same direction as his line of sight and as gargly as they had sounded. The Gilbertese helmsman gargled back.

"Water in the fuel. Another 20 minutes."

I asked him about Ocean Island and the Phosphate Commissioners who mined it. Making the best of a bad job, he spoke at length.

"You'll be posted here one day likely as not and you'll find what most people do. The day in the office - off to the club for a few cheap beers - home with too much liquor in you and fall asleep in your chair before going to bed. That's 5 days a week. On Saturday or Sunday you have a game of tennis or a swim in the manager's pool if the great man favours you, perhaps a film or a party in the evening and then more beer - twice as much as during the week. Year in, year out with as little change as the climate, sitting on the same dusty heap of tropical paradise and only looking forward to your leave in Australia. None of these people have been to the group - that's the Gilberts - most of them have never been round Ocean and most of them never go on the sea nor get to know the Gilbertese or Ellice."

He paused, wrinkling his face with the intensity of his speech. He turned abruptly and pointed. "See that ruined jetty?"

A tangle of rusted girders had come into view as we drifted.

"Yes" I said.

"That's the old loading area. Blown up in the war before the Japs came. And those cliffs."

"Yes".

"That's where the Japs stood the people they shot - or bayoneted - you fell over the cliff and saved a burial. And this sea" - he waved his hand towards the west - "that's unknown to them, how to live off it, how to survive on it. They talk about it in the club and it's the same old stories going round and round but they know nothing and they do nothing. They don't look, they don't search, they don't experience and they don't learn the history. They would have to walk or bicycle - there are only four private vehicles on the island - and that's too much effort."

He waved at the west again: "It is 2,000 miles to the nearest land. Nothing but empty sea but a Gilbertese travelled it in his canoe during the war - 7 months in a 9 foot canoe. Those people who go to the club see him every day and they know his name and what he did. But he can't understand much English and they can't speak Gilbertese except to count the beers they want so they know what he did and that's about all. You'll probably meet him. Certainly if you are here any time. Nabetari he's called."

Hamish was interrupted by the helmsman. Evidently the engine was clean and he wanted to know whether he should change the fuel. "Yes". The fuel tank was drained into an old tin, and rinsed.

I commented that there was nothing to see, certainly no water.

"Only a few drops and it's at the bottom of the tin. We'll fill it up with clean fuel and hope we'll go."

So did I. We were well clear of the land and the prospect of 2,000 miles in an open boat did not appeal. But we started easily and I lay flat on my back on a seat until we reached the jetty.

"I should very much like to meet Nabetari" I said to the policeman.

"That will be easy but as you don't speak Gilbertese you won't learn anything from him and he doesn't like questions. I am giving you dinner tomorrow - D.C. will do you today - so we will talk then."

The following evening I dined with the Chief of Police. We ate outside on a patio and looked west over an ocean flecked with spots and stripes from stars. Occasionally a brighter light from a fishing canoe moved across the scene. Palms swished gently and from time to time loud squawks came from a tree nearby where birds were roosting. I reminded him about Nabetari.

"Nabetari?" He said as if he had never heard the name. "Have you met him?"

"No. Only two clerks in the District Office and neither of those had that name. Where does he work?"

"Well, you will meet him. He is a steward in the B.P.C.[2] mess. Nothing to look at but a very ordinary Gilbertese just like all the others you have seen."

---

[2] British Phosphate Commissioners

He paused "Funny life. Works inside all day, fills up the fatties with beer in the evening and never goes out, except to Church on Sunday. But he has probably had enough of the great outdoors for one life." He thought a minute. "Well, let's start at the beginning."

"Nabetari was recruited in Nikunau in the southern Gilbert Islands in 1939 for work on Ocean Island. Nikunau has a lagoon and on lagoon islands they have sailing canoes so Nabetari could sail and he also was a good fisherman. He had had a good education from the missionaries and he could read and write Gilbertese and understand English. His education probably got him selected for work but he came to earn enough money to build his own canoe.

"The Pacific war started in 1941 and the Phosphate Commissioners were told that Ocean Island would not be held against a Japanese attack so early in 1942 they destroyed the loading gantry and wharf and took up the deep-water buoys. Most of the Europeans went to Australia and some of the Gilbertese were taken back to their islands but many remained and a few Europeans opted to stay. In the middle of 1942 the Japanese took the Gilbert Islands and arrived on Ocean Island.

"The Europeans were put in gaol, where they lived for two days before being bayoneted. The head-quarters of the occupying force was established in the District Office and the Japanese soldiers were billeted in the houses of the Europeans who had worked for the Phosphate Commissioners.

"The Stores were commandeered by the occupying forces and any work a Gilbertese was required to do earned him nothing except abuse.

"Before European traders established themselves in the Gilbert Islands in the nineteenth century, building a canoe took many years and an enormous amount of effort. Not only are there no suitable trees on the islands for making timber but there are no materials for making tools. For the manufacture of a canoe, pieces of driftwood had to be gathered when they washed up on a beach. They came from South America 5,000 miles away. To cut the driftwood one had to use fire or a sharp stone or sea shells. Then, as today, the wood had to be sewn together with coconut fibre string, threaded through holes bored with sharp pieces of shell.

"Sitting in shade a Gilbertese boat builder spent years putting together his odd shaped pieces of wood.

"Knives in most Gilbertese eyes were the single greatest benefit brought by European civilisation. For canoe builders it was sawn timber. To be able to buy timber of any length, width and thickness was the fulfilment of a dream and to be able to cut it and work it with saws and drills was the fulfilment of a second less vivid but still remarkable dream. A dream, which for Nabetari and many others, was realised by working in the phosphate fields.

"Nabetari had bought his wood and started to build his canoe before the Pacific War started. Now that there was no employment he had time on his hands and work on his canoe went quickly so it was finished a month or two after the Japanese arrived." The policeman paused. "Like all canoes, carvel-built, planks sewn with coir recessed into the wood, painted smooth, the lee side flattened and the hull very slightly bowed. That way they sail better.

"The Japanese made the Gilbertese fish for them. This was not without its hazards as a poor catch was rewarded with a beating while two Gilbertese who had caught a tuna and secreted it were found out and shot.

"As the war continued and the Japanese suffered defeats they adopted a two pronged and nonsensical policy towards the Gilbertese. They taught them the use of fire-arms so they could help resist any invasion of the island and they treated them with ever less consideration. For not bowing to a Japanese or not bowing satisfactorily a beating with a rifle butt was common and any breaking of the curfews was punished by shooting. Floggings were also given. A Gilbertese was chosen to administer these. He used a cat - a stout stick with 6 knotted cords bound on the end. The cords were stiff and tarry and the knots gave them weight. A dozen lashes turned a back into mince meat. One Gilbertese who refused to lash a friend was beaten with rifle butts until his head was pulped. After that no Gilbertese refused to give a lashing if ordered and acting as executioner was not held against him.

"In 1943 the Americans staged the first amphibious assault of the war in the Pacific and captured Tarawa, the head-quarters of the Japanese in the Gilbert Islands." The policeman paused again and added "Well protected by British naval guns taken at Singapore.

"On two square miles of land 7,000 Japanese and Americans died in 3 days fighting. Thereafter other islands were easily freed and the Americans built 4 major airfields to receive supplies and as bases for bombers. A reconnaissance plane was probably sent the 250 miles to Ocean Island, as soon after the landing an aeroplane with American markings flew over. A few Gilbertese were turned out, given their rifles and ordered to shoot.

"By deducing that the plane must have come from Tarawa the Gilbertese realised that the Japanese had been defeated in the Gilberts and the allies occupied them.

"Nabetari was using his canoe with a friend, Reuera. They usually went out with two other canoes in a group.

"They talked:

'The i-Japan are bad. We are all dying.'

'Yesterday Bauro was shot.'

'For what?'

'He took some tea for himself when he was cleaning the officer's house. Buren and Meritera threw the body in the sea.'

'And Bitiare died two days ago. He was stuck with the long knife on a gun.'

'We shall all be dead and fed to the sharks. Everyday they come to see it there is anything for them.'

'The i-Matang are in Tarawa again. We must go to the Gilberts.'

'There are no sails.'

'We can paddle.'

'It will be four days.'

'Against the current.'

'Yes, but it is weak, and we can do it.'

"So they agreed to go. On a moonless night they loaded the canoes with young drinking coconuts and dried fish, then carried the canoes from the top of the beach down to the reef and launched them. They paddled quickly away from the land heading south before turning east. There was a black-out on the island and they all remarked that compared with the time the Europeans had been there even the land was dead. But they did not look back and paddled steadily to the east into a faint breeze. It was April 1944.

"They did not know what chance they were taking. The highest point on any island in the Gilberts is not 10 feet above sea level and that point is on a man made mound. The islands are small and scattered and to try and paddle to one in a canoe from 250 miles away is like firing a bullet into a high flock of birds thinking you will bring one down or perhaps throwing an electron into an atom and thinking you will score a direct hit in the nucleus.

"From only 6 or 7 miles away in a canoe can you see an atoll. Some Pacific Islanders study the waves in the open sea and after half an hour or so can say in which direction land lies. But the Gilbertese do not have that skill. Out of sight of land you hope for birds to guide you or if you are lucky with the clouds you may see the greenish reflection from a shallow lagoon.

"For a day and a half the three canoes paddled east. They were cheerful at leaving Ocean Island and the soldiers of Nippon and had plenty to eat and drink. Then the trade winds started to blow. Steadily from the south-east without gusting and without stopping. The canoeists paddled against them and seemingly made way through the sea faster than before. But the harder paddling tired them and they knew, although they could not see or sense it, that the current, wind driven, would be flowing against them at 3 to 4 knots. They agreed to turn round and go with the wind.

"The paddlers could have been hopeful, if unreasonably so, of finding one of the 16 Gilbert Islands when they went east. The chances of returning to Ocean Island were infinitesimal. The island is approximately one mile across and even though it is some 120 feet high unless one came within 10 miles of it there would be no chance of seeing it. However, in Gilbertese legend there is further land to the west - the land of Matang whence their ancestors came, ancestors which they believed to be white so that today the name for a European is an i-Matang. "One from Matang". The canoeists thought perhaps this land would be a few days past Ocean Island and they would reach it. Certainly there is land to the west but the nearest big area is New Guinea and that is 30° of longitude or at the equator some 2,000 miles from Ocean Island. In Atlantic terms from the coast of Ireland to the coast of Newfoundland.

"They stopped paddling except to guide the canoes and make sure they did not drift apart.

"One morning early, before the sun had hauled itself above the horizon, Nabetari heard a shout. His body was stiff like it always was after a night half sitting, half lying in the canoe and he wriggled those parts which were not rigid to sit up. A man in another canoe was standing up, a dark silhouette on a dark sea cutting the line of the horizon.

"The standing man shouted again and, turning his head again, Nabetari looked where he turned. There was no third canoe. The Pacific was very

28

calm. No breeze blew and the surface of the water was smooth and unwrinkled but tilted very slightly and for a great distance like a long field of dark slate. The canoes were edging up the slate and when they came to the top it would be like reaching the ridge of a roof and they would see briefly roof upon roof for miles before sliding down with the roofs disappearing and they reached another trough from which they would again be slowly heaved.

"Nabetari took his legs out of the bottom of the canoe and carefully crouched on the struts. He spoke to Reuera as he watched for hundreds of yards the rising water coming towards the canoe.

"Tebao's canoe has gone."

Reuera was half asleep and grunted.

"Which way?"

"We can't say which way, we cannot see it."

"As the canoe neared the top of the swell Nabetari stood upright and looked over the sea. He could see into the trough that was going and beyond to the horizon and into the trough that was coming and beyond that to the horizon and a long way along his ridge in one direction and a long way in the other direction. But beyond the ridges, although the sea looked flat Nabetari knew that it wasn't and although the other canoe was probably one or two miles or so away he would never see it unless it reached the peak of a swell at the same time as his own canoe reached a peak. But he looked, and although he knew the other canoe would never hear, he shouted.

"That night and every night thereafter the two canoes, 30 or 40 yards apart, tied themselves together with a line until one morning there was no other canoe and Nabetari and Reuera were alone.

"They looked and they shouted but they saw nothing but the sea and heard nothing but their own breathing and the lapping of water against the canoe. It was difficult to imagine what had happened to separate them. If the other canoe had started to sink they would have heard shouting.

"If it had suddenly capsized they would also have heard it. As they had been tied together and were drifting in the same direction how could they get so far apart that they could not see or hear each other? Nabetari and Reuera were Protestant Christians, taught by the London Missionary Society, and in the evening at length they said prayers with great devotion. But they knew about the old gods of the Gilbertese, the spirits of the land and sea and the ghosts that can be smelt but not seen and heard. So when Reuera said that the sea goddess Teanti had opened the water and let the canoe fall silently to the bottom of the ocean Nabetari understood him and was frightened. That evening they prayed with fervour for protection from such a fate and during the day they wondered where the other canoe was going and whether the men were paddling.

"Some days later or perhaps a week or two, Nabetari could not remember well but it was not as long as a month as they were cutting a notch in the gunwale at full moon, the canoe over-turned. It was night and he was asleep in the back of the canoe. As it tilted he was being pushed by his weight against the side of the canoe and he saw above, long and black, the float of the outrigger.

"Since he was a boy he had been in capsizing canoes and he knew that the only important thing to do was to hold on to the canoe so as not to be hit by the outrigger as it came down. If you were thrown into the water before you could hold on then you stayed under the water for as long as you could. As the canoe went over he missed his grip so he dived. When he surfaced he looked around. The canoe was hull up, white in the dark sea, and he swum to it and held on to the outrigger frame. He looked about but saw no Reuera. He shouted. Again he shouted but no voice answered. He swam around the canoe thinking that Reuera might be unconscious in the water and from the other side of the canoe he shouted. He neither found Reuera nor heard him. He thought he should swim away to find him but which direction and how far - and he could lose sight of the canoe and then he would be lucky to find it again. So he held on to the canoe, shouting every few minutes.

"The sea is indifferent to life. If an animal swims or drowns it makes no difference. If an animal lives and draws nourishment from the waters or dies and adds nourishment to the waters it makes no difference. The sea is a soup taking waters and minerals from the earth, concentrating them, separating them, building them into small knots of life, the small knots forming masses engulfing other knots and masses until they emerge supremely strong and active in the seemingly dead liquid as a whale or great shark only to collapse and unravel into the million constituent parts from which they came. Some of the knots of life by-pass the race to size and singly as anemones or collectively as coral live immensely long in a slow paced unadventurous existence. So is the sea biologically patient but physically the sea is no slow creator and leveller. It can be infinitely placid or infinitely violent and is always infinitely different.

30

"It is calm or rough, lazy or ferocious. Sometimes lapping shores and beaches; other times hurling against rocks or cliffs and destroying them. It takes away rubbish and cleans, and it builds up banks and shoals and sinks ships on them. The sea is blue and smooth, the sea is white and foaming; it is unheard, it roars above the greatest noises of man; it heals sores and sickness, it tears to shreds and fragments. But the sea is driven by the wind. On its own the sea does nothing. It is placid and calm. But it is a woman with a neurotic dependent personality, the mistress of the wind, and at the command of the wind it changes its personality, lies to be caressed, dances with joy, heaves in sullen temper or shrieks ferociously and demonically in tantrums of destruction. The command of the wind makes it the great Hindu god Vishnu but it is Vishnu the destroyer as well as Vishnu the preserver.

"So it was now with Nabetari. Short, sharp waves driven by a squall had over-turned the canoe and thrown the two men out. For a time the canoe sunk beneath the heavy waves and with difficulty heaved up like an injured beast huffing and gurgling for its life. Then the wind died and the waves changed. They raced and leapt forward, flecked white, rushing past the canoe into the dark like young dogs on an unending hunt. They nuzzled up to the hull and ran into it with light slapping noises and nosed along the timbers and swirled in eddies and the canoe became alive shaking itself and resting in a trough before moving on the slope of the next wave until it reached the top and shuddered and panted before it started down again, wishing to join the hunt and race off into the night with the young smiling dogs - dogs which called and encouraged it and wondered perhaps, having seen canoes sail, why it would not lift itself on the water and prance with them to the horizon and beyond.

"Nabetari took stock of his situation. What was left of the equipment? He hung back on the outrigger and put his feet into the canoe feeling for any floating object. He moved along clasping a gunwale, one foot up in the hull. He found neither paddle, nor coconut, nor fishing line. A piece of thick string rubbed his shin. It was tight and not floating free and he realised it was the cord tying an old jam tin to a thwart.

"He had the bailer! Probably the most useful piece of equipment of all. He slid his fingers along the string making sure it was not frayed or cut and tested the knots on the tin and on the wood. Then he left the tin to dangle in the sea and continued to search with his foot. He found nothing but on the outside of the canoe his hand touched rough coir and he realised the drain hole in the hull was still plugged.

"In the area of the Gilbert Islands the Pacific is between 2,000 and 4,000 fathoms deep, say 2 miles to 4 miles. Floating on the surface of this abyss attached to his fragile craft Nabetari hung like an insect blown on to a lake or pond and like an insect he was succulent. A large shark could take a leg off in one pass. A barracuda with fast dashes and snapping jaws could tear him to pieces in minutes, shreds of meat and blood spreading into the sea with each strike. In the southern islands of the Pacific divers darken the soles of their feet or cover the soles with leaves so that the paler flesh thrashing in the water does not look like a wounded fish. The Gilbertese do not do this but Nabetari thought it best to keep very still. For a long time he waited in the dark. When the sea had quietened he started to right the canoe. He stood on the outrigger and sunk it as deep as it would go. Then he put his arms over the canoe and grasped the gunwale on the side of the outrigger. Standing up with bent knees he kicked the outrigger away and leant back hauling on the gunwale. Slowly the outrigger passed under the canoe and rose until the float reached the surface. The air that had been caught in the hull escaped as the canoe was righted and full of water it lay, the sea almost lapping in. Very slowly Nabetari turned it until it was bow on to the waves. He then worked his way to the stern, took up the jam tin and started to bail.

"It took a long time to get the water out. It was not possible to put any weight on the canoe and Nabetari had to hold an outrigger strut with one hand merely to steady himself while bailing with the other. As the canoe slowly rose the outrigger gave more support but he had to lift himself higher to reach over the edge and into the hull. Eventually, when there was freeboard of nine inches or so, he stopped bailing and moved to the middle of the outrigger framework and next to the canoe. Watching the sea and making himself ready to drop all holds and fall into the water should a large wave come he pulled and pushed himself up and over its edge. Without resting he bailed furiously until the canoe was floating high and light then he moved to the stern and more slowly scooped up the water in the bottom, taking care not to rub his tin on the planks and damage the string binding the planks together. Twice more in the night he had to bail and realised the canoe was leaking.

"When the sun rose he took stock of his situation.

"His sole equipment was the canoe, the jam tin and his lavalava. He had no paddle, no fishing line, no hooks and no clothes. He had no food, no water and no shade from the sun. On the equator, hundreds of kilometres from land, he was alone in a 9 foot canoe. The current which carried him was moved by the wind. If the wind dropped the current slackened. If the wind went round to the west the current would stop or reverse its flow. To the west of Ocean Island the equatorial current averages one kilometre an hour.

"As the day went on and the sun got hotter Nabetari became more anxious, more depressed and ever thirstier. He wondered whether Reuera was still swimming and he stood up on the canoe to look for a dark blob of a head upon the sea. He wondered whether he should not choose a quick death and drown himself. He used a finger to collect the sweat off his body and put it in his mouth. The taste was foul and he spat and rinsed his mouth in the sea. Late in the afternoon he started to pray. He felt better and when the stars came out he felt they were God's candles and they were lit to cheer him.

"The next day was still and hotter. The sea was almost flat and in the heat acquired an oily creaseless look, heaving slowly and regularly as if asleep. The only breaks in its surface came late in the morning when flying fish popped out of the water in batches of two and three, spread their fins and sped fast and shiny in all directions, going like rockets and hitting the water fifty yards away with sharp splashes. The flush continued for some minutes and one fish landed in the sea near the canoe. Nabetari thought he might have hit it if he had a paddle but it swam out of reach and as the sea rose it jumped out of a crest, beating its tail and bent double, then straightened its body, put its fins out and sped away.

"Only very rarely is the sky clear in the central Pacific. The norm is for small puffy cumulus clouds to float across the blue coming from the horizon and disappearing to the horizon in a casual drift, wistful debutantes without partners. Above atolls and islands from mid-morning to the evening they are pushed off course. Hot air rises to many thousands of feet from the land and the clouds are thrust aside to left and right. Ill treatment for so many girls in their gentle passage across the heaven!

"If rains fail the land dies under the equatorial sun and the rising thermals divide on-coming clouds even if clumped in great masses. The land dries, the drought worsens and the thermals strengthen further. A massive onslaught of rain is necessary to break the cycle. Ocean Island has had droughts of seven years.

"But sometimes the white clouds cluster over the horizon, scowling and darkening and rolling into banks that cover the sky for miles. Against the blue and over the blue they come grey and evil looking, skin tight and swollen obscuring the sun and their shadows chilling the air. Then the darkest, blackest cloud may split vomiting its rain into the sea and over the land. The heavy speeding blobs will be lost in the water but spread over the soil in rivulets and the people and the earth, sandy as it is, will be pleased because there is never enough rain on the Gilberts.

"The second day after his canoe had capsized Nabetari saw a cloud with rain beneath pouring into the sea. He tried to judge its path and used his arms to paddle the canoe towards it. But his paddling was feeble and tired him so he stopped. He waited and saw that the cloud would come over him so he bailed the canoe out. Quickly the rain approached. When it was 100 metres away he heard it hissing on the water and saw it turning the clear sea murky. A sharp gust of wind blew. The rain approached rapidly, the sea went grey and then it was falling on the canoe. Nabetari missed the centre of the rain but for a quarter of an hour he enjoyed bliss. He opened his mouth to the drops, swallowed them and rolled the water round his cheeks and tongue. He held out his cupped hands while keeping his head back and drank the rain he collected. He pushed his fingers through his hair and washed his arms and face and legs in the rain, holding these parts over the side of the canoe. Never in his life had he felt so cool and fresh and clean. As the rain died away he took the jam tin and filled it from the bottom of the canoe. Then he drank as much of the water in the canoe as he could. It was brackish and fishy but palatable. Clean, no longer thirsty and much cheered he sat and watched the rain cloud getting smaller and fainter as it moved away over the ocean.

"Two days later it rained again and on the following day Nabetari had his one crucial piece of good luck. He was looking at the sea when he saw the fin of a small shark. The fin was moving slowly, circling the canoe. Nabetari set about attracting the shark. He wet his hands in the sea and then rubbed them hard on the outrigger framework where fish had been dried. He put them back in the sea and washed them clean, then rubbed the outrigger again. He repeated this and saw the shark was circling closer. He saw its body and judged it to be not more than two and a half feet long. He put his hands in the sea and thrashed the water to make the shark think there was a wounded fish. He rubbed the outrigger and washed and thrashed his hands again. The shark came closer. Nabetari wet the outrigger well so that water dripped into the sea and rubbed his hands hard along the outside of the canoe, hoping that there was a taste of fish and that it would bring the shark up to the canoe. Then he lay still, his hands over the side above the sea. The shark circled the canoe more slowly and then swam towards it. Slowly it followed the path through the water which the canoe had made in drifting. It reached the stern of the canoe and paused. Then, touching the canoe with its body, it moved forward. Nabetari waited until the shark was beneath him at the middle of the canoe. Very slowly he moved his hands down. Two inches above the shark he stopped. Then he seized it. One hand grabbed it in front of the tail, the other went over its gill slits and held it tight against the canoe.

"The shark bucked and wriggled. It snapped and tried to turn its head. Nabetari got a finger into a gill slit and rolled the shark round slightly. He pressed it against the canoe so that the gill slits not covered by his hands were tight against the wood and slid the hand which had held the tail up the body of the shark. He put his hands together over the gill slits and covered them to stop water coming out. He hoped the shark would not be able to breathe. He held and waited and pressed, balancing the canoe, watching the shark and watching the sea.

The shark thrashed the water with its tail and tried to wriggle out of the man's grasp. Nabetari held firm. He hoped no other sharks would hear the commotion and come to investigate. For an age he held. His arms got tired and he tried to press ever harder. The shark's struggles weakened and eventually it was still. Nabetari kept holding and waited. Then, when he was sure it was dead, he moved one hand back to the tail, put the fingers of the other hand into the gill slits and lifted the shark out of the sea. He put it in the bottom of the canoe and then stretched and exercised his arms and body. When he had rested he tried to tear the shark.

"The skin was tough and without a knife Nabetari found it difficult to open. He rubbed the vent with the rim of the bailer and managed to bite off a piece of flesh. He chewed this slowly while he worked. He lifted the shark and opened its mouth, taking care not to be bitten by any nervous snap. He forced the mouth over one of the poles of the outrigger frame where it extended across the canoe and started to wriggle a tooth. Backwards and forwards he pushed and then twisted and turned. Eventually it came loose and slowly and patiently he used it to cut up the shark. Some of the skin he left in large pieces, some he cut into strips. The flesh he hung on the outrigger frame or on the gunwales. It took a long time.

"Nabetari made a cup of a piece of skin and bailed out the canoe. Then he used skin to stuff a leaking seam and stopped water coming in almost completely. The insides of the shark he examined and found two small fish only slightly digested. He removed these and set them out to dry. The remainder of the insides he threw away. Bones and fins and the head he kept.

As he worked he chewed more flesh, extracting the juice and spitting out the pulp. When he had finished his work, he washed in the sea and drank a little of the fresh water in the bailer. Then he rested.

"The shark provided the means of survival. The flesh fed Nabetari and from the bones he made fish-hooks. For a line he untied a binding on the outrigger and unravelled one of its skeins. In case the outrigger was weakened he bound the joints with strips of sharkskin. With a piece of skin as a lure he trolled and caught fish. It rained and water collected in the canoe. Nabetari filled the bailer and covered it against the sun with a piece of sharkskin. For some time after a heavy shower he could drink the water in the canoe. But slowly it got too fishy or too salt to be pleasant and he had to bail, using again a piece of sharkskin. When he had no water he relied on fish he caught for moisture.

"So it went on day after day, week after week, month after month. Ten to twelve miles a day the canoe drifted west. Not that Nabetari knew that it was west because the canoe could point in any direction, turning as the waves and swells deflected it. Over the months the sun moved from north at noon to south at noon so it gave no indication of compass bearings but he believed it would be west as that was the way the sea moved about the Gilbert Islands.

"Nabetari spent the day sitting. In the very early morning as he lifted himself out of the bottom of the canoe the sun warmed him and loosened his muscles, stiff from the night. As the sun got hotter the wind blew on him, keeping him cool and his hair, which grew long over his shoulders, kept the sun off his skin. He watched the sea to the horizon for ships and land and nearer for birds and fish and as the sun got higher and hotter he just looked at the near water where red reflections ran along the backs of the waves and wondered whether he would live. He saw two Japanese ships and he lay down in the canoe and hoped he would not be spotted and he saw two American planes and he stood up and waved but they passed over. In the late afternoon he lay down in the canoe, partly to keep warm and partly to watch the sun set with its reds and oranges and darkening blues and purples which slid over the waters behind him from the east.

"The night he loved. The million stars twinkled and shone quivering from the sea and he could wait and watch for the moon shining half the nights in the month. Happily he saw it grow night by night until it was full and lit the rustling water. Sadly and regretfully he watched as from being full at sunset it rose uglier and later each night until it reached half moon. Then it slimmed to a crescent until shortly before dawn one day he knew he would see nothing until 5 or 6 evenings later, when facing the other way the crescent would appear above the sunset.

"As the last light of the sun paled on the horizon Nabetari said his prayers. Not to himself and not really aloud but in a gentle murmur and in time with the tapping of the waves on the hull so sometimes the prayers came a little faster or a little slower than at other times. He thanked God for his help and asked that it would continue and that he would also help the friends with whom he had left Ocean Island if they were still alive. Then he asked God to look after his father and mother, and his grand-parents and brother and sisters and he went on to pray for his pastor and his church on his island and that the fishing might be good and he prayed for the people he knew on Ocean Island to be kept safe from the Japanese and for the British and Americans who would come one day to free them. He thought he should also pray for the Japanese as he had been taught to pray for his enemies but he could not do this as the Japanese were cruel without sense and had taken away the dignity of people he knew and liked and this he could not forgive.

"When he had finished praying he usually ate fish and either drank water or if he had no water chewed the flesh of a freshly caught fish and sucked as much liquid out as he could before spitting the pulp into the sea. Then he lay back and watched the sky and dreamt, bringing up images in his mind as he willed or tried to will.

"On his island there was a road which lay next to the lagoon. It was the only road on the island and as there were no cars and lorries it was used only by bicyclists and people on foot. It was hard and firm and a yellowish colour and over-hung with coconut palms which cast on its surface slow moving grey shadows. The road entered a village where small raised platforms made of laths and with thatched roofs stood in the shade on both sides of the road. The platforms were on short poles and were arranged in pairs, one near the road and the second behind and his family pair was the fourth on the right. He could see under the tied up blinds where he sat next to his sister to the next hut and to another and another where old people and young people sat talking or got up to tend fires or feed a pig in a pen of logs. At night the village was mysterious with oil lights shining on brown skins and from the dark voices suddenly laughing or calling to a fisherman who had come in with a catch.

"Nabetari's parents and grand-parents were alive and like all Gilbertese he respected them, particularly the men, and would have done anything he could for them, but his grand-parents were old and reminded him of death and his precarious situation. The thought of the life and activity of the village disturbed him so his mind slipped away to the lagoon which glittered along the edge of the village where the children played and the fisherman sat in canoes. But the image reminded him of his life imprisoned on the vastness of the ocean so again his mind slipped away and he thought of his church and the silence when the pastor on Sunday told them to contemplate and pray without speaking.

"Another evening he walked along the island road to the end of the land. He came to a finger of white brilliant sand beyond which the sea foamed and surged and two men in canoes bucked up and down. He had heard it whispered that it was here the spirits of the dead left the island and travelled over the ocean northwards, island to island on the way to their new world. The thought of the open sea and the dead brought him no comfort and his vision left the noisy scene to the space and peace round his church where there were a few tall palms standing in clean grey gravel and no sound from waves smashing on reefs.

"In the centre of his village was the island meeting house, a high building of poles and thatch with the roof coming near to the ground so one had to stoop to enter or leave. The meeting house was the centre of community life and there were strict rules for behaviour and only a few old and respected men were allowed to speak publicly. The house was quiet and cool and he liked the idea of sitting in his family's place and watching and smelling the old men smoke and listening to the quiet gossip. But then he came out and the light was so bright that it hurt and there were people coming and going, and from the lavatories that stood out in the lagoon on stilts came loud shouts from the users complaining about their constipation and diarrhoea. He thought it noisy and trivial and his vision slipped again to his church.

"He thought then of the Government Station which he knew was important and which he much respected. Prisoners from the gaol swept and re-swept the sand and white-washed and re-white-washed the surrounding wall, and the head of the well. The island magistrate in a heavy blue lava-lava and white shirt with a big shiny buckle on the belt where shirt and lava-lava joined went in and out of his office and talked to people who came to see him. Occasionally a komitina (commissioner) came on a boat with all the children running away shouting "i-matang, i-matang" and spent days talking to the

38

magistrate and the old men of the island council. But then the komitina left, the magistrate had a rest and the Government Station was empty and the rope to the flag flapped against the pole all day without stopping and the flag cracked like a whip in the wind and he found that pointless and annoying so he went back to his church. And the church was tall and white and rectangular and had windows of beautiful coloured glass, the only glass in the island and inside it had rows of seats and they were the only seats in the island and they were polished shiny brown like the pulpit. At the far end of the church which faced the rising sun, although to point the shortest route to Jerusalem it should have faced west, was an altar with a metal crucifix and shining brass candlestick and a thick cloth of blue lined with red and worked with silver thread and Nabetari had never seen metal so beautiful, for he only knew saucepans, knives, fish hooks, screws and nails, or cloth so splendid and they stood in his dream under the window of red and blue and yellow and green and which surely was the inspiration of God. And when he left the church and looked at the building with palms bowing above it he thought it the finest building there could be and if anybody had spoken against his church or his God he would have fought them and killed them if he could, so strong was his pride. And sometimes in his visions the Church was filled with people all dressed in white who sang to wonderful tunes and described a world he only knew from the words of the pastor and the reading of the bible. For there were no hills, nor green fields nor grass in his life nor eagles nor deer nor lions, but only squawking sea birds and dogs and cats and pigs, and images and dreams of his church, which in the evening he thought sat on the sea a little way towards the horizon slightly dimmed in the haze, and brought him much contentment.

"One morning, as Nabetari was sitting watching the sea, he saw gliding 100 yards above the water a large black bird. As he looked it flapped its wings and with the movement of its body he saw a red patch on its throat. Frigate bird.

"He was tired and semi-comatose. The months in the canoe had made him weak and listless, otherwise when he identified the bird he would have shouted and, being religious, prayed with fervour, for frigate birds roost at night so land had to be near. As it was he was comforted and said to himself, without speaking, a prayer of gratitude.

"The next day and the next he watched the clouds to the west. He looked for a tinge of green which would mean a lagoon. Instead on the third day he saw a grey streak on the horizon. Slowly over the hours it thickened and then, quite suddenly, a line of light appeared under the grey and above the sea.

Nabetari knew he was looking at palm trees and as he came closer the trees turned green, the line of light disappeared and a white sandy beach took its place. Very slowly the canoe drifted into the shore.

"Nabetari had watched the land approach as if in a dream. But he knew he was not dreaming but rather seeing himself from above. He was separated from his body, watching himself in his canoe as it approached the land. His life on the open sea was slipping away and like somebody dying he was coming to a new life which was infinitely more beautiful and in which he would be absolutely at ease. He realised he knew this life from long ago, it would be familiar and comforting and he looked down on his body in the canoe thinking of it escaping from purgatory and wondered, although he knew what to expect, what the new existence would be like.

"He saw the sea below the canoe lightening very gradually to a paler blue. Then at the limit of vision, as far as he could see into it, it turned grey and he recognised the floor of the ocean was rising. In long minutes the sea slowly went blue-green, followed by clear and the floor below turned white and then gold. Some silver fish swam beneath the canoe followed by shadows alternately hidden and heightened by the crossing grey or bright lines cast by the ripples of the sea. The canoe started to pounce on wavelets running in from the ocean and then the bow jolted and stopped and the craft slowly moved round and beached along its length.

"Nabetari watched himself lying in the canoe as at the edge of the surf it rocked gently on the sand. He saw himself wondering whether he wanted to leave his old life and the 9 foot trench with curved sides that had been his shelter and support, it seemed for ever. But he realised he did not like the movement of the canoe and the sun was getting hot and it would be cooler under the palms above the beach, so he started to move his body and as it used its arms to pull it up, he re-joined it and together they climbed over the edge and fell through the water on to the sand. He sat up and holding the canoe, tried to push himself upright but his legs were weak and he realised he could not stand. So he crawled and left the sea. The sand was cool near the water's edge where the wavelets chased up and down but, as he moved up the beach, it became hot and burnt his palms so that he made fists and crawled on his knuckles. He reached the trees and sparse coarse grass and crawled to a trunk that was in shade and sat with his back to it.

"He rested and looked at the beach below him, his canoe white and neat at the edge of the water and the sea blue to the horizon. The scene was familiar and reassuring so with the rustle of the palm leaves fronds above he wondered if perhaps the past months were a dream. Then he thought he must return to the canoe and fetch his dried fish and the water left in the bailer. So he turned round and balanced on his knees and grasped the trunk of the palm as if to climb it. If he could pull himself up he could walk. But he could not. He could only squat and then get no higher. He tried again pulling up on the trunk and, trying to push with his legs, he held himself as close to the trunk as he could and turned his head and as he did this he saw some three trees away a sight so bizarre and unexpected that he knew he could not be dreaming. Scattered about were American sweets, some loose and some in tins and among them were de-husked coconuts. He knelt, holding the palm, and with his head bowed, prayed to God for this last great kindness and told Him, as God knew, the sweets were like the colours in the window of his church at home.

"Nabetari drank from the nuts and ate sweets and then he slept. He woke and drank and ate. Then he went to a palm and holding on, tried again to stand but be could not and collapsed. He crawled down the beach, past the canoe, and into the sea until he was floating and his outstretched arms were nearly at full length with hands in the sand. Turning west he pulled himself along parallel to the beach.

"Late in the day he saw a man walking in the bush above the beach. Nabetari was too weak to feel strongly about anything but he was surprised and rather shocked to see that the man was black and he waited before he called hoarsely at him. The man called back and then came down to the sea. They couldn't understand each other but the man motioned him up the beach and indicated he was going away and would come back. When he returned he had three other men with him and they carried Nabetari to a village." The policeman paused and we were silent. After a while I asked.

"Where was he?"

"In the Ninigo group - that's part of the Admiralty Islands north of New Guinea. It was November and he had been seven months in his canoe.

"There were Americans all over the place and they put him in one of their hospitals. He was in poor shape and unbalanced but he recovered quickly and told intelligence about the Japanese on Ocean Island. Then he hung around for some time and learnt to cook and eventually came back here with the first Americans. He was scared to land, in fact I think they were probably all scared as it was a ghost place. There was nobody alive and the Japanese were

41

lying in groups, except for single officers and senior N.C.O.s in houses where they had slit their stomachs, their bodies dried and wrinkled, with ghastly wounds and clotted blood. Not a single Gilbertese did they find. They must have all been killed on the cliff top and thrown into the sea. But the houses, the village and the warehouse and offices were neat and clean. In all senses the island was dead and we have only Nabetari's account of what happened along with the Japanese records."

The policeman finished his story and we sat without speaking, drinking whiskey. Finally, he spoke. "Tomorrow's range day. Would you like a pull?"

Enthusiastically - it would be much better than sitting in the District Office and reading the codified laws of the Gilbert and Ellice Islands Colony - I said "Yes" and paused "And Nabetari, is he all right?"

"Seems so but he doesn't talk much and I do not think he has ever been back to Nikunau".

The shooting range was on the north of the island. Its greatest length was just over 100 yards and on one side was a mined area where phosphate ore had been hacked out with picks and shovels from between very hard coral pinnacles. The coral was dazzling bone white as was the range which ended at a cliff top, beyond which was the sea and the horizon.

A squad of police were being drilled. They stamped to halts, turned left, right and about and covered their boots, stockings and shorts in grey dust. The Gilbertese sergeant was strict and had two men he condemned as being "Idle on parade", doubling to the end of the range and back, carrying rifles in two hands in front of them and with faces rapidly turning as grey as their uniforms and marked with glistening blobs of sweat.

As I watched the men drill and then lie down to shoot, I had a flash back of myself as a ten year old. I was learning to shoot with a 22 on a 25 yard range and drilling in dust on a play-ground with, as a treat, a 303 fitted with a Morris tube to take 22 cartridges held on a shoulder. The ex-RSM who took us spent much effort and suffered much irritation - but used no army language - trying to get us to "form fours". Rifles waved in the air or clashed together as we shuffled, many different sized boys with different sized steps, to somewhere near where he wanted. But I could not remember the command to un-form fours and get into two lines when he would spend a lot of time getting the lines straight. It was all a waste of effort as by the time I was a soldier we marched 3 abreast, never two or four.

42

As soon as I lay down and took up a rifle all that had been told so many times came back. Two sighting shots, the second a magpie and then into the bull, and the best target of the day earning a laconic "Quite good, my boy" from the policeman. News of my shooting, trivial as it was, spread at a rate that was astonishing.

I was having a quick sleep before supper that evening when a ghastly howling woke me. Stumbling to the window I looked out and saw, half way up a sixty foot coconut palm, a Gilbertese climbing happily upwards and singing his heart out.

I asked my host about him at our meal.

"They howl to frighten off the spirits when they cut toddy. That toddy cutter was telling the spirits he would get the new commissioner to shoot them if they didn't leave him alone and give him lots of sap." I felt very flattered.

The next day I got on a boat for Tarawa. The policeman came on board to talk to the captain. When he had finished I said good-bye and thanked him for looking after me. Looking at some sailors lounging on the deck and speaking sideways, he said "If you ever hear anything of security interest you can let me know. Don't write but I come to Tarawa from time to time."

It took a day and half to Tarawa, plunging into a swell. The ship lifted and fell sharply and as the only alternative to sitting in a hard chair at the table where we ate I lay on my bed. This was screwed to the after deck above the rudder and propeller and was open to the weather with rusty railings holding three sagging wires to guard against a Pacific ocean that tried frequently to rise to my height and haul me away. I thought of Nabetari and my first experiences of colony life on Ocean Island. There were not any startling conclusions except that I respected and liked the Gilbertese, was undecided about the whites in their various nationalities, and disliked small boats. More positively, since the day I had landed on Ocean Island I had gone on to full pay!

3. GILBERTESE PORK

For the first two weeks after arrival in Tarawa I was quartered with a well organised bachelor whose household produced good food on time. He appreciated my needs better than I and before he moved on, leaving me his house and his office, his cook had found me Timeon and his wash girl had found me a wash girl "Uareti" (wireless). Timeon, I was told, had worked in the bachelors' mess on Ocean Island and was a "good cook". This was something of an exaggeration, rather Timeon was a good opener of tins and managed well for two weeks on the food I had brought up from Australia - tinned hams, stews, meat balls, vegetables and fruit. When he had repeated his opening up and heating up cycle of tins three times in the two weeks I told him to cook something else.

"What?" he asked.

I thought hard and simply.

"Macaroni cheese. And make it brown and slightly crisp on top."

Came supper time and Timeon advanced from the kitchen splendidly smart in a white shirt and starched white lavalava and put a steaming dish on the table. I took the lid off and saw that while it was nicely brown it was not the shade that one expected. It also looked rather wet. I spooned out a large portion and tasted. Timeon was standing nearby.

"Is this the pudding? It is very milky."

"No. Not pudding. Main course."

I tried again.

"Timeon, what is in it?"

He looked at the ceiling, scowled and recited.

"Onions, bovril, macaroni, sugar and milk I make from powder."

Two days later, when I had my first supper party, he served toad in the hole, to the Yorkshire pudding part of which he had forgotten to add any flour.

The guests were very polite.

"Best sausages in custard ever" and "full marks for imagination".

Nobody could recommend a better cook and I liked Timeon who was helpful and, going into his trance and scowl mode, told long stories of Gilbertese life and legend and recited generations of ancestors' names. But the stock of tins from Australia was going down quickly and with Timeon's help I decided to explore the possibilities of my islet.

The next Saturday I started at the liquor and food section of the Wholesale Society store, the only shop on Tarawa, jotting down prices as I went round the aisles.

Beer at one and four pence a large (26 ounce) bottle was a quarter of the value of potatoes at two shillings and sixpence a pound, taking into account that half the potatoes were obviously bad. Whisky at eighteen shillings a bottle was cheap too on this comparison, while onions, the only other fresh vegetables available, were three shillings and four pence a pound. Also half the onions seemed bad. Everything else was in tins and packets and after travelling 3,000 miles from Melbourne, being unloaded at Ocean Island, stored for anything up to two months, loaded for Tarawa and stored again ended up three or four times the price in Australia.

The manager of the store came up to me while I was doing my round and offered advice. He was very helpful and after a short talk on what the store had to offer and a long talk on the history and the prospects of his rugby club in New Zealand, I asked him if he had any meat in a freezer somewhere. "No", he said, "We don't have a freezer, but if you go along the lagoon road to the gun emplacement at the end of the police lines you will find the butcher's shop open today."

Arriving at the emplacement I came upon a small collection of children and dogs, a drooping Vickers 6 inch gun leaning out of a ruined pill box, part of a pig hanging off the end of it and a large Gilbertese with a panga standing above more pig on a flat piece of crumbling concrete. The panga came down with enormous force on part of the rib cage, a piece of meat flew off and was grabbed by a dog, the nearer children acquired a spray of blood and the butcher swore.

The children shouted "I-matang" and the butcher turned round, greeted me with a dazzling smile and said "Welcome to my store. Sir."

I introduced myself as a customer and asked him what he had for sale. He moved over so his slab was visible but it was very difficult to distinguish one piece of mauled meat from another. The part of the pig hanging from the gun looked a better bet and I asked if he could cut some chops. He looked puzzled and had to be given an anatomical explanation. He smiled, said "Yes" and started to let the carcase down. It was not a good idea I felt to stop and watch the chops being prepared so I contracted with a child to bring them to my house for 6d and left the scene.

Half an hour later the small boy and a friend arrived with a green basket woven from a palm leaf. We put the basket in a large bowl and left it for Timeon.

The previous bachelor had kept chickens. Timeon had raked up the top layer of the run and put all - I hoped - enriched soil in a crate, some that was left over went into a small trench. Doing my daily inspection I was most excited to see the spinach I had planted coming up in the crate and the 6 tomatoes in the trench were doing well. Now that a butcher had been located, I thought on Saturdays there shall be good food. Pork chops or even a roast leg - which would make the main course for a meal with friends - with fried tomatoes and boiled spinach. A healthy meal of fresh food with plenty of beer to wash it all down.

Timeon came out and told me lunch was ready.

"Did you cook the chops?"

"Yes, I fried all the chops."

So I went in noticing a delicious smell in the house and sat down.

Timeon came in and placed on the table a large heap of the reconstituted dried potato that was so unlikeable, if filling, disappeared to the kitchen and came back with a plate from which rose something like the bloody hand of Ulster, pointing upwards out of a carnage of bone and flesh. But, more realistic than the heraldic hand, it was haired and hooved.

"Don't put it down" I shouted. "take it to the kitchen and I will carve there."

A close look at the meat showed three rib bones, part of the shoulder and a section of the leg joined by very fat flesh and long sinews.

Knives proved useless and slow.

"Timeon, lend me your panga and bring the hammer." Laying the sharp edge of the panga on the meat and holding it steady Timeon hit the blunt edge with the hammer and we slowly hewed off pieces of flesh. It was very under-cooked.

"Fry it again and when it is cold put the rest in the refrigerator." Twenty minutes later there was another call to lunch. The small pieces of meat were nicely browned, perhaps rather fat, but smelling delicious. I took my first fork load, chewed and spat. Beneath the brown it was pure rubber, flavoured with coconut and fish, the fish flavour dominating and definitely nastier than the coconut.

Timeon explained.

"All Gilbertese pigs eat coconut and fish. Nothing else. This one mostly fish. Not many coconuts on Betio."

"Open a tin of bully beef, Timeon" and he left with something of a smile while I went for a whisky - cheap at any rate, I thought.

Saturday, two weeks later, I had eaten my whole crop of spinach and tomatoes. Approximately 6 leaves and 1 small fruit. The spinach showed no sign of producing more leaves and the tomatoes obviously were in the course of departing this world. Sympathetic friends told me that if I really wanted to grow anything my name had to be down on the soil list. When a government boat came from the Solomon Islands it always brought 100 bags or so of soil. Half of this went to the Residency and the rest was divided among Government officials in order of their seniority. Nobody actually said that as the latest arrival the bottom of the pecking order was my place, but they did point out the house would not be mine "for ever". The half bag of soil or so which would be my ration would I imagine produce perhaps two tomatoes and it would be my luck that they would be green but on the point of ripening when an order would come to move elsewhere. They would have to be left for some predatory friend. Unless of course they could be made into green tomato chutney but then it was certainly not possible to buy the other ingredients of chutney whatever they were. So I decided to give up gardening or almost. The District Commissioner heard of the matter and man to man told me "Plant paw-paws. They will grow. Put them in above your septic tank and pee on them every night. You will get fruit in 6 months."

I followed his advice and it worked but rather quicker help came from Timeon. In talking to him I asked about getting fresh fish. All the Gilbertese ate fish and it should be possible to buy some. He looked rather aghast and said there was plenty of tinned fish in the store and that tinned salmon and pilchards in tomato sauce were very much nicer that anything that could be caught in the sea. When I disagreed with him I could not make out whether he was shocked at my proletarian taste or by a general lack of appreciation of good food, which had to qualify as such by being tinned. There was always, he said, tinned fish available in the mess at Ocean Island, as if this were the Maxims or Tour d'Argent of the Gilbertese world. Then he thought. There were, however, many various foods that could be obtained for me from the reef if he only had a light. I replied that he could borrow one of the pressure lamps from the house and that I would come with him on the reef. This proposal rather put him out but he cheered up when I agreed that I would hold the lamp while he wielded the knife.

The Tarawa lagoon is triangular with land enclosing two sides and a submerged reef the third. My house stood at the end of one side of land where it met the reef. At low tide I could walk across sand to the lagoon or, further, where the reef was uncovered, to the open ocean. At high tide the lagoon came to within six feet of the house, being barred from the living room by a row of small boulders, and stopping four inches below the floor.

The first high tide I experienced made me think the house and contents were likely to take off, and with me hanging on, disappear and sink. But soon I became accustomed to the tides and took to regarding the lagoon with a friendly interest and as an ever present clock.

When one heard the sea slopping on the boulders, a pleasant noise which reminded one of boats and rivers, it was high tide and as I would otherwise be in my office, it was Saturday or Sunday afternoon and about tea time. If I heard it at night it was 3 or 4 o'clock and there were some hours of sleep to come. At low tide there was silence and stretches of sand to be seen so it was near mid-day or mid-night. At neap tides, a week earlier or a week later, the order of highs and lows was reversed.

Seawards there was always something of interest on the reef and the sea that covered or did not cover it. From low tide when the water was distant it moved shorewards, hiding the dazzling whites and yellows of the sand with a veil of pale blue that was laid slowly and darkened and thickened as the water deepened. As the tide rose, the shallows by the house acquired shadows that ran across the sand from the ripples and wavelets above. These took dizzying intricate patterns when the moving water hit the boulders and ran out to sea at an angle across the incoming waves. Sometimes a fast little sand shark flashed yellow and brown as it skimmed over the bottom making for the shade which a few palms cast where they leant over the beach. Even the sun-baked boulders outside the living room came to life when the sea reached them. A multitude of small red hermit crabs crept out of crack and crevice, crawled lop-sided in the shells they wore and slowly climbed slopes of stone

48

and sand. Otherwise these crabs came in only at night when they crossed floors and climbed the walls making scratching noises or falling occasionally with a clink on the concrete. Sometimes they were in great numbers, spotting walls and floors with red, and their soft noise filled the house. Birds also watched the lagoon. Grey and white reef herons crouched along the edge of the water and small white terns fluttered over it diving for fish. When the reef was uncovered at low tide golden plovers, travelling on their migrations between Australasia and Siberia, appeared at the equinoxes and poked curved beaks into the sand. They were the only land birds in the Gilbert Islands.

On first arrival at Tarawa I had swum above the reef with a spear-gun. But I was a poor hunter and a worse shot and the only fish that I ever hit was a box fish. Box fish are coffin shaped with fins, head and tail added on the body like unplanned extensions or superfluous ornaments. They swim very slowly and rely on being poisonous for protection. It was no great feat to kill one and when I next swam on the reef and did not see a fish in the pool where I had killed I felt sorry and, as there did not seem anything large around, gave up spear-fishing.

I had also bought a canoe. It was an Ellice model made crudely from a hollowed out tree with an outrigger and did not like to paddle straight. When a friend going on leave lent me his Gilbertese canoe and I learnt to sail, the Ellice canoe was stored away and I gave up crab-wise paddling to speed out to a small uninhabited islet in the lagoon that was only ever visited by picnickers.

Swimming on the reef was a delight although it could not be fitted in every day. The water would be in the eighties and vigorous exercise was exhausting so floating around with a mask and doing a few dives became the rule. I always drank a mouthful of sea water thinking of all the trace elements being absorbed and not present I suspected in Timeon's cooking, and sometimes wondering whether my body would learn to accumulate gold, or, rather disturbingly, uranium.

On Sundays I walked out with goggles to the corner where the beach joined the sea reef. There were corals in many varieties and colours with brilliant fish, dainty or lithe, hovering among them. There were also the remains of a landing craft wrecked in the invasion of 1943, where large shell fish grew and other fish swam fast in and out of port holes and the gaps in the iron work.

So the reef was of beauty and interest and, if Timeon was to be believed, it was to be a larder as well.

It was a night or two before the new moon showed when we went on our expedition. There was still light on the sunset horizon and Timeon said we should wait until it was darker. So we sat on the boulders outside the living room. I had the pressure lamp and Timeon used its light to sharpen a panga. His only other equipment was a palm leaf bag and a piece of stout wire about two feet long. It was bent back at one end to form a hook and both the point of the hook and the curve of the bend were sharpened. I asked what we were likely to catch and he tilted back his head and stared at a star. Screwing up his eyes he uttered gutturals of Gilbertese out of which I could only recognise the words for a ray and an octopus.

Betio village was to our left. Fishermen were going out for the night carrying their canoes and shouted at each other and to their families left behind. Dim yellow oil lamps and a few bright pressure lamps shone from the huts under the trees. To our right was the flashing red light at the end of the mole and beyond it the lights of two ships anchored in the lagoon. A rusty tank was in front of us, resting tilting on its wheels with a broken track, its gun pointing out to sea.

Fifty yards away two people with a light appeared on the beach and Timeon said we should go. I picked up the lamp and we walked out on to the wet sand, Timeon saying it would be a good idea to start by seeing if anything could be found by the tank. At the back of the vehicle he stopped at a shallow pool, scooped out of the sand by water trickling out of the hulk.

"Hold the light as high as you can."

I did so and Timeon bent over until his face was about a foot from the surface of the water and studied the bottom of the pool. After half a minute he tensed, raised his knife and then cut through the water into the sand. The pool became murky and we had to wait for the sand to settle. There were two halves of fish and Timeon picked them up and put them in the leaf bag, then exchanged the knife for the wire and used it gently to poke the bottom of the pool. There was a sudden flurry of sand and another flurry of sand at the further side of the pool. Timeon changed back to his knife and cut into the second flurry. Two more halves of small fish became ours.

"Nothing else here." he said. I lowered the lights and looked beneath the tank. There was a large pool between the tracks.

"What about that?" I said. "You could crawl in."

He looked.

"No. There may be a moray eel or even a sting ray. One must not put a hand in such places."

"I want to look inside the tank before we go."

I climbed up on the body and leaned into the open hatch of the turret. The breech of the gun was open and shells in their cases were clipped round the inside of the turret. The tops of the shells had rusted away and the noses stuck out on stalks from yellow explosive and brown metal.

"Oh. A crab." Timeon was beside me and pointing down. I moved the light and saw on the floor of the turret a big blue crab. He had his claws down but his stalky eyes were bent towards us trying to see what was behind the light.

"I will get him." said Timeon and started to climb on to the turret.

The shells next to each other on the turret walls with detonators in their noses were only too obvious and certainly in an unstable state after years in sea-water.

Timeon's knife if it hit them would speed us both to join their former owners in the next world.

"No" I said and explained the danger. He only grunted and was, I think, more impressed with the loss of the crab than the possible loss of his life. We moved out on the reef and left the soft sand near the beach to come to areas of pools and weeds in spongy compacted masses. We reached a pool with stones in it and crevices in its sides.

"We will try here" said Timeon.

He put the knife on the reef and knelt down above the pool. Taking the piece of wire he slid it slowly into a hole and when it was in as far is it would go he twisted and prodded gently.

"Nothing" he said and pulled the wire out.

He tried another hole and then another.

"Ha. Rock cod" he said.

He pushed on the wire and then gave it a sharp thrust then twisted it before pulling it slowly out. Impaled on the end was a small, blotchy, brown and white fish.

Timeon took hold of the fish by its underside and as he touched it the fin on its back rose with a row of spines sticking out of the membrane. "Well avoided" I thought. The wire was pushed through the fish and it was dropped in the bag.

He tried other holes in the pool and found another fish. He asked me to lift the light higher and bent over to look at the bottom. He rolled over a large brown sea cucumber which squirmed and ejected a cloud of sand, then putting down the wire he picked up the knife.

Taking a large stone carefully by its side he lifted it. A browny yellow eel slid out. The knife splashed and left it tailless and writhing. Timeon changed to the wire and impaled the front part of the eel, then chopped its head off and put the body in the bag.

"Moray eel?" I asked.

"Yes, moray eel."

"I thought they were poisonous and could not be eaten."

"No. They are good but the skin is poisonous and you must take it off carefully. We rub the eel in the sand to do this. It is also not good to be bitten by one. That's why I cut the head off. I won't cut myself on the mouth if I put my hand in the bag."

He bent over the stone which had sheltered the eel and lifted it right up. There were two whelk-like creatures in shells which he picked off the bottom. More carefully, for it has a poisonous bite, there was a speckled cone shaped shell which he removed.

We left the pool and in a meandering path followed the retreating tide.

There were lights from other gleaners on the reef around us and the flashing red light at the end of the mole was now to our north. A stretch of dark water lay beyond the reef in which the reflections from the anchored ships gleamed. Far away the light at the end of the Bairiki pier also flashed red and behind us were the lights of Betio unevenly grouped. One or two bicycles were moving on the road and the lights of the club shone brightly, its generator put-putting sharply.

As we walked Timeon turned over stones and prodded in weeds and holes.

No pool, however small, was left un-investigated. Some small fish and a couple of eels were his reward. He also found some more shell fish. Three or four times he saw bubbles in the sand and, moving quickly, thrust his wire down where the bubbles rose. He caught nothing. At last he was lucky. He thrust the wire down by some bubbles and it held something. Keeping the wire firm he asked me to dig with the knife. I put the lamp down and did so. A long yellow worm was my reward. We also found some small clams, buried in the sand with only the edge of the shell showing.

We came to a big pool and Timeon carefully turned over a stone. He peered for a moment and then said "Rika" (octopus).

I looked but saw nothing. Timeon explained its position to me. I looked again and saw a pale fleshy brown blob flattened over a large pebble. Tentacles spread out from the pebble almost matching the sand and very difficult to see. Two small eyes looked at the light from a point near the junction of the tentacles with the body.

Timeon put his hand in the water above the octopus and moved it slowly down. Suddenly the octopus gathered itself into a lump the size of a tennis ball and with its tentacles streaming behind shot away, leaving a dark cloud of ink where it had been. I swung the lamp over so we could follow it. It settled gracefully at the side of the pool where rock met sand and moved half under a small ledge. It spread its tentacles, those holding the rock changed colour to match, the rest of the octopus remained the colour of sand.

Timeon walked round the pool until he was above the octopus. He knelt and carefully put his hand in the water, moving slowly down. Near the octopus he snatched quickly and caught the body. With a tug it was off the rock and out of the water with the tentacles waving in the air, showing rows of suckers underneath. Timeon raised the octopus and twisted it so that he had the eyes next to his mouth. He then pressed it to his teeth and gnawed it.

Against the brown skin of the Gilbertese the octopus became almost transparent and pale pink. Mauve blue streaks showed in its body. The suckers on the tentacles palpitated and were the colour of raw pigskin and leathery looking. As the tentacles waved some clamped on Timeon's face. He took no notice but shut his eyes and bit harder into the bag of soft looking wet flesh he was pressing against his face. Suddenly the tentacles dropped and Timeon took the octopus from his mouth. He lifted it up to show me and I saw a nick between its eyes where he had bitten it. He dropped it in the bag.

"Is that the easiest way to kill it?" I asked.

"Yes. You must bite only between the eyes."

"Can't you stick a knife in?"

"No. It may miss the place and you can get ink over everything.

"Isn't it unpleasant?"

Timeon looked somewhat astonished.

"Unpleasant? No. It is quite easy. You can do the next one."

What a fool I was to have said so much! My stomach tied itself in a knot and I had to swallow hard. I breathed deeply and shook my head.

"Hold the light up, please" said Timeon, "and keep it still."

He was searching the pool.

I held the light with both hands and over where he was looking.

"No more octopus please, no more octopus please", I said to myself. "Please no more octopus," and there weren't. He found some shell fish and said there was nothing else. We moved on and I breathed freely.

"You must only be careful to shut your eyes when it is near your face and to hold it so that it cannot bite you. The bite is bad."

My heart sank again.

"You think it is quite safe for me to try? I have had no experience with octopuses."

"Yes. All Gilbertese children do it. You must just be a little careful."

Timeon spoke with the same lack of interest that I might have used in telling somebody I would show him how to get into a car when he saw one for the first time. He would not think it was disgust or fear if I did not try the approved method of killing but rather a childish sulk. It would have to be done.

We approached another pool. I held the light up and Timeon prodded and searched. Two small fish but mercifully no octopus. No such luck at the next. He moved a stone and there, sitting under it, was my octopus. He was sandy coloured and was too dazed by the light to make any attempt to move when Timeon put his hand through the water. He caught it and held it up. It was larger than I thought.

Timeon put his wire down and took the lamp. He held the octopus out to me "Hold it as I am" he said.

54

I wiped my hands on my shorts, clenched my teeth and stuck out my right arm. As I got near the octopus put out a tentacle on the back of my hand. In a reflex I pulled my arm back. The tentacle held firm and the octopus was nearly pulled from Timeon's grip. He laughed.

"Don't you like it?"

"No. It is very strong and rather slimey."

"It is like a fish. Only its mouth can bite. Now hold it above my hand." I put my hand, opened, over Timeon's, the tentacle twisted the skin, then came off. My fingers open, I hovered a moment then with great determination grasped the top of the octopus. Like a balloon filled with water, it gave as I pinched it and blew out beyond the grasp of my fingers. Tentacles writhed wildly.

"You are holding too hard" said Timeon.

I relaxed my grip. The blown-out section of octopus subsided, sliding over fingers and palm. I felt as if I would have to throw it away at any moment.

I slid my grip down until my hand was touching Timeon's. He took his fingers away one by one until only his little finger and thumb were round the octopus. I tightened my own little finger and thumb. The octopus slid up through my grip. Timeon let go. He put the lamp down and prised two tentacles off his hand. They hung down but one and then another of the other tentacles rose and gripped my wrist.

"Now raise it to your mouth and bite" said Timeon.

"Yes."

I raised the octopus and brought it slowly and reluctantly towards my face. Four of its tentacles had now found my hand or wrist; the two Timeon had taken off his hand hung limp and the last two writhed and curled.

I took it away.

"Where are its eyes?" I asked.

Timeon looked at me with wonder.

"You must feel for them."

"I squeezed my hand and tried rubbing my fingers on the octopus.

"No" I said, "I can feel nothing."

"Let me look and I will tell you."

Timeon parted my fingers and looked at the octopus. He told me the eyes were between my first and second fingers.

I lifted the octopus bending my wrist. I slid my fingers apart and saw the eyes. I hesitated, then shutting my eyes brought my hand up to my mouth. The flabby bag pressed against my lips. Two tentacles at least grasped my face. I opened my mouth, sucked and bit. The skin was tough. My front teeth felt as if they were biting rubber. I moved my teeth so that I was biting with my eye teeth. Another tentacle fastened across my face and forehead. My arm started to shake. I ground my teeth. I shut and bit harder: I felt something on my chest.

"It's dead" said Timeon.

I took the octopus away from my mouth. It was flaccid and looked small.

"Take it" I said and quickly, before I was sick, I knelt and scooped salt water to my mouth and washed my face.

When I had finished Timeon was unconcerned and waiting to go to the next pool.

"Timeon, that is a Gilbertese thing to kill an octopus. I am not doing any more."

"All right, Sir" he said and we left the pool. We wandered about on the reef, keeping as near the line of falling tide as we could. Timeon said it was time to smoke and we sat down. He produced tobacco from a tin and while he rolled a cigarette with a piece of dried leaf I sat and looked at the sky.

The heaven was vast and into it were fitted stars that were larger and brighter by far than the small points of light that shine in the nights of Europe. So expanded and numerous were they that it looked as if we were beneath a vast mosaic dome built with diamonds, blue and white, flaming opals and rubies, but stones had fallen or been lost and some were dim so that there were dark holes and patches and the dome appeared old and in poor repair. But enough stones remained and enough stones were bright to show the former glory and one felt the blackness was new and intrusive and wished for a celestial workman with hammer, cement and sacks of gems to put back the missing stones and clean and polish the ceiling to the brilliance it had been.

If above the sky was bright and alive the damp sand underfoot was dead. The sea had slunk away and the only water that remained, trodden out of the sand, filled foot prints with reluctance. Where had the sea gone that had given life to the lagoon that was so familiar to me and which had supported and nourished the animals we were chipping off rocks, cutting with a knife and spearing with wire? In my fancy it had deserted our victims and, ashamed, was creeping over the edge of the land to the outside submerged reef where it slid down the side of our island's pinnacle to join the somnolent cold and dark waters at the bottom of the sea which supported a very different life.

Timeon finished his cigarette and we continued our meandering progress along the low tide mark.

Then, quite suddenly, a ripple of water wet my shoes when it should not have done and I realised the tide was coming in. We should have hurried to hunt more beach before the water covered it but I had stepped into the incoming sea and found it cool, when it had been warm, and animated when it had been dead. Phosphorescence flashed round my feet and when I stopped and kicked a brilliant shower of sparks streamed out, with smaller sparks rising from fallen drops. I asked Timeon to take the light and moved to where the sea was dark and in excitement and pleasure kicked again and again to produce displays like trailers from exploded rockets.

So I walked, splashing and watching the water as it ran in rushing into small depressions in the sand, filling them, mounting the far ridges and flowing over into the next hollow. It was a great invasion of wavelets and streams separating and coalescing to fill an empty waste.

"Where had it come from?" I wondered and thought of my earlier speculations. As it was cool it was not from the surface and must have come from deep in the lagoon or, deeper still, from the open ocean on the far side of the reef.

If it were lagoon water it was returning to where it had been a few hours before and, remembering the warmth it had enjoyed and the crevices in the coral in to which it had run, had come back with eagerness to re-experience pleasure and the excitement of exploration.

If it were water from the open ocean it was coming to an existence that was new, hurrying to leave the cold still depths where the only light came heatless from luminous misshapen fish, and was moving tentatively and then ever faster into an unknown world. For six hours it would flow into the great bowl held on its pedestal of coral, disappointed perhaps at first by the dark of night but then the water would be pierced by the lights and colours of the rising sun and it would run up the beaches blown by the dawn breeze and tumble and jump in the wild dance of the breaking surf. So the rising tide answered my speculations and told me it knew where in the sea it would like to be.

Timeon was far along the beach, half bent, holding the light up with one arm while he chopped into a pool with the panga and reluctantly I left the excited water to join him.

The bag was filled with small fish, more octopus, shell fish, sand worms and a mullet we found in a pool and chased to exhaustion. This was our biggest catch and must have weighed a pound.

At the house we tipped the contents into an enamel bowl in the kitchen. Timeon asked me what I would like. It looked a most un-appetizing catch. Flabby pieces of worm and octopus were mixed with chopped fish, eel and dull looking shells. I said he could keep the lot except a clam which I wanted to try.

I went out on the reef many times thereafter but I never went again with the idea of getting food.

4. THE AUDIT CAT AND A DOUBLE DOCTOR

I was a bachelor and there were definite advantages to this condition. After the early trials with Timeon we had worked out between us a satisfactory diet based largely on fish, all shapes and sizes, supplied to us by locals supplemented by coconut sap (Toddy), pasta and tinned orange juice. This largely Gilbertese style diet was pleasant and healthy. However, many of the Europeans, particularly the women, could not get used to such a menu and lived on tinned food which consumed a great part of their income. So I was relatively well off. A second advantage of my bachelor state was that married men at some stage or the other got involved in the inter-wife quarrels which for women with nothing to do and a servant or two to help them do it were always simmering. No third party likes or dislikes interfered with my acquaintanceships and friendships.

Lastly I was allocated the cheapest and most run down accommodation available for expatriates. My houses were built of laths and poles without nails and tied together with Gilbertese string. There were no ceilings and steeped pitched roofs soared in all rooms to a lofty apex. The "walls" for the rooms were 7 or 8 feet high and the only security provided for the larder was chicken wire spread across the top to stop anybody climbing in. A friendly prisoner emptied the lavatory bucket and no heating was necessary for the shower where the water was kept by nature at 80°. It contrasted well in comfort with the brick and fibre-board of the newer Government houses, favoured by most wives. These had tin roofs, suffocatingly low ceilings and were built in clusters so that they could share septic tanks. A breeze through such houses was hard to come by but mine were always cool.

The only inconvenience of my houses were the glassless windows. These not only let in the spray from the lagoon, but also cats intent on perpetrating or evading rape.

There was a shortage of cover for them in our sandy, near bushless, world and as the new houses could be secured against access they chased through and round mine, howling and mating under the beds. Most of the cats I recognized, seeing them as quietly meowing animals in their owners' houses and then again by torch light as banshees crouching in my shower or bedroom with an air of ferocity for which their dear owners would never have given them credit. Some I managed to hit with whatever came to hand or to wet with a glass of water when they would run with all carnal desire quenched, except that is for the audit cat who, even if drenched, would glare and spit before vanishing with dignity out of a window. He was called the audit cat as he was a badge or appurtenance of office of the Colonial Auditors who only did one tour of duty in the Colony as a precaution against any fraudulent relationship developing with the accounting staff. This cat lived in the house allocated to auditors and was known as Tom Fell Bell Quantick reflecting his sex and the succession of owners. He was large and of a shiny Nubian blackness. One ear was torn and only a stub of the other remained. He was much scarred, a lightning raider of larders, broad in the shoulders and chest and lean and lithe in the rear. His eyes shone like a pair of sodium lights, he walked with a swagger and a flicking tail and the strength of his smell would have been the envy of any lion, there being no vets in the Colony to counter such matters. All other toms gave him his distance and he had a list of females whom he raped by rota. His children must have been drowned in dozens. The first time I identified him in my house he was making off with a rat, he stopped and scowled, waiting to see what missile would come his way and my shout of "There's a good cat" must have come as a surprise for the scowl was extinguished and, in no hurry, he disappeared outside.

Some six months after my arrival on Tarawa, the fashionable opinion on Tarawa was that the cats round the European houses had reached plague proportions. Houses had to be shut tight at night, howls kept people awake, catty smells proliferated and any food not closed in a refrigerator or a meat safe disappeared without trace. "Cats must be shot" was the universal consensus but as nobody wanted their cat shot or a friend's cat shot it was also the universal consensus that the new cadet who had no cats or female alliances should do the shooting. He was also told he had a reputation as a good shot.

To make sure that blame or social stigma would not come my way I mentioned my "hunting" expedition to the Resident Commissioner. He said "Excellent" in the hearing of a large number of people and with my social rear thus protected I organised a shoot. The Assistant Accountant General lent me a 22 and ammunition and, sliding his eyes to their corners, said he thought the first cat to go should be that "big shiny tom without an ear". Recognising a political motive I agreed for diplomacy but told the auditors wife that the cat should be shut up for the shooting season as I did not wish to shoot it by mistake.

Six cats were shot and Tom Bell Fell Quantick lived on and became Tom Fell Bell Quantick McGillivray, but his harem, at least temporarily, was much diminished. Unfortunately in due course I had to move out of the shabby, comfortable and large houses into the brick and fibre cells of the modern houses and disliked them as hot and restrictive. In such an agreeable climate when one could sit out all night under the stars or all day under palm trees shutting oneself up in a box seemed nonsensical. Luckily though I went often on tour - travelling to and staying on islands away from Tarawa - and without exception the rest houses on "outer islands" were built of Gilbertese materials with each having its own character and peculiarities.

The hospital on Tarawa, two hours across the lagoon from Betio, was moved and the island government took over the wards and houses. The Senior Medical Officer's house was declared the rest house for touring officials and I often stayed there. It was under the shade of close set palms and tall pandanus trees and stood at the edge of a passage leading from reef to lagoon, in the deepest of silences. No sun fell on it and the walls were dark and damp and fallen leaves and coconut fronds covered the ground around, giving off a faint smell of decay. In the lagoon end of the passage was a small island which supported the sagging poles of a bridge. When the moon was full and rose early in the evening it glided up large and smoky between palms. For a time it was obscured by fronds before moving clear into the sky where it shrunk in size and took a cold hard sheen glittering on the waters outside the house.

Stone fish were found in the passage. Squat blotched little fish, they are invisible on a rocky bottom. If trodden on, a spine on the back pierces the sole of any soft-soled shoe and goes deep into the foot. Poison is injected and may kill. At the best there are days of intense pain followed by a slow period of healing. No European pain-killer is of any avail but the Gilbertese have a remedy, known only to a few, which reduces the agony. Swimming in the passage one always jumped into a pool under the bridge - not to touch bottom - and came out on shallow sand.

While the picturesque passage and its rising moon compensated for the gloom of the Tarawa rest-house, the gloom of two rest-houses on islands in the central Gilberts was unmitigated. These rest-houses were on the islands of Abemama and Aranuka, almost on the equator, and ruled in the late 19th century by a king whose tyranny has been described by a number of visitors, the best known being Robert Louis Stevenson. The King, Tem Binoka, was pictured by Stevenson as an intelligent man and a despot with no regard for life. Rifles he bought from traders were tried on his subjects. He liked difficult targets such as a sailor at the top of a swaying mast-head and with his policy of extending royal ownership of land and enforcing punitive taxes he succeeded in reducing the population of Abemama to a tenth or a fifth of what it was at the start of his reign. This remnant could be considered lucky for he conquered the neighbouring islands of Aranuka and Kuria and caused the entire populations to flee. The land registers on these islands when I visited them showed 80% of the land as owned or recently owned by Binoka's descendants. On both islands the inhabitants were all of immigrant stock, many on Kuria being descended from a Scotch administrative officer, George Murdoch, who had retired there and had taken up procreation as his main activity in old age. Having a government pension he was among the richest residents of the Colony and could afford many women.

The heir to Tem Binoka had married one of George Murdoch's daughters. Among the offspring of this union was the King of Abemama and a brother who became an assistant district officer in the Colonial government.

Both these men kept as far away from their patrimony as they could. The king married the high chieftainess of Nauru and went to live on that island and the brother secured dispensation from the government from ever having to go on tour to Abemama and its dependencies. However, he realised well the odium in which his family remained in the southern Gilberts and when he stayed at the rest house on Onotoa he put the Union Jack to protective use.

The Gilbertese attached great significance to this flag and it was for them the symbol of British rule. When the Royal Navy established a protectorate in 1893 and declared peace upon the islands, interrupting an intra-island war on Tarawa, they erected flag poles and flew the union flag. No doubt the hauling up and down of flags on ships and shore by their new rulers impressed the Gilbertese and the taking down of flags at sunset and their raising in the morning was exactly observed at all government stations.

Desiring to enjoy the sexual offerings of Onotoa and bearing in mind the jealousy of the Gilbertese where their women folk are concerned the assistant administrative officer took maximum precautions. To guard himself and two girls he had procured he posted four island policemen outside the rest-house for the night. He also brought to the house the Union Jack from the Government Station and hung this as a canopy over the carnal bed. Guarded by island police, the crosses of St. George, St. Andrew and St. Patrick and no doubt locked doors, His Royal Highness enjoyed his pleasures.

The rest-houses of Abemama and Aranuka were as gloomy as their inhabitants. The Abemema rest-house was in the middle of the island and had no wind and no view but mosquitos in plenty. So bad were they that at night, tightly buttoned at throat, wrist and ankles and wearing boots one either lived in a cloud of insecticide sweating on account of the amount of clothing or got into bed under a net.

A trader in the past had introduced frogs to the island with the intention that they should eat mosquito eggs and larvae in the watery babai pits in which they breed. However, while the mosquitoes were not appreciably diminished by these predators the Gilbertese were extremely upset. The croaking and splashing of frogs at night filled these undoubtedly brave sailors with fear and in my days it was against the Laws of Abemama for a frog to be introduced to the island.

On Aranuka, an island over-grown with unkempt bush, there was a dingy rest-house standing raised on the side of a sheltered lagoon. Its sole attraction was the view at night.

At low tide the lagoon had only a few inches of water over a large area and like Timeon and myself many people went fishing with knife and light. A few fishermen used paraffin fuelled pressure lamps but most used the fronds of coconut palms rolled up with constricting rings to keep them tight. With a ring in place at the top of the leaves they smouldered red. Sliding a ring down and swishing the six foot roll through the air broke out a fire and you had a torch flaming above the holders. The lights spread over the lagoon moving haphazardly, occasionally coming together and then parting. Bodies were only partly visible, a head or the side of a torso or a limb, or, as the knife man bent, a back. The pressure lamps made brightly defined silhouettes and the flares softer blurred lines kinder to brown bodies. From pools in the rocks and the water of the lagoon the lights were reflected. There was little wind at night but the movement of the tide and ripples from the sea produced long reflections. The widest part of the reflection was always towards one and as it extended away it diminished to a point. In my fancy I saw in the lagoon from the flames many Malay krises shining and waving. Or if I looked beyond the top of the reflections there were dark gaps and then the lights of the flares or lamps. The gaps became settings and the lights precious stones. The steady glare of a pressure lamp was a diamond. The long jumping flames of a flare a star, sapphire or tiger's-eye moving, as the stone was turned in one's hand.

The gloom of the island and its history had seemingly affected the people who lived there. From the Magistrate down they were a lugubrious lot and I left the island with joy.

My pleasure at going was heightened by the anticipation of the canoe voyage which we were to make to Kuria. The Government viewed such voyages with great disfavour in view of the expense of looking for craft which had gone missing. Colony ships had to search millions of square miles of ocean for a missing fisherman who might merely have gone to see his family on another island, usually with no success, while for a missing boat the New Zealand Air Force would send up Sunderland aircraft 1,500 miles from Fiji to search even more ocean, also with usually no success. Permission was only granted for our voyage with great reluctance as no ship was available and on strict conditions as to the safety of the Government money we carried in cash and postal orders, the safety of other Government property and lastly, the safety of ourselves. With the trade wind behind us we sailed the few miles from the dark green jungle of Aranuka, looking rather like a shaving brush jutting out of the hole it had made in a blue cloth, towards a stain of syrup, Tate and Lyle gold, on the same blue cloth which, with ragged green crest behind the stain, was Kuria. We were a pretty sight with our white sails and hulls, and to remind us that we were indeed on a voyage in the South Seas a large shark was cruising off the entrance of the boat harbour at Kuria when we arrived. The dorsal fin was cutting the water in best story book fashion and it jumped once half out of the water to show head, mouth underneath and a long elegant body.

Kuria was two islets. Each was triangular with points touching in a narrow neck of sand. At low tide the land changed shape. The neck widened and uncovered sand extended in a plain from the side of one triangle to the side of the other making a rectangle. This was the golden stain we had seen from the canoe and the rest-house was almost in its middle facing from one island over the neck to the second island.

The rest-house was on the site of George Murdoch's house, and, having travelled the Gilbert Islands for most of his life, he had chosen the finest situation in the Colony on which to build. The south-east trades blew steadily but not strongly through the gap between the two islands to cool the house, the outlook took in the acres of sand, covered by water at high tide of a particularly brilliant blue, there was at a comfortable distance a view of palms and thatched houses to the left, and to the right of the Pacific to the horizon. As the incoming water had so much sand to traverse high tide gave the warmest swimming in the Gilberts, temperatures being in the 90's and small fish of colours one did not see elsewhere hovered in pools, one species with a blue flash along the length of their bodies nibbling at my legs and refusing to flee despite loud shouting and violent splashing. It was a delightful restful sea-side cottage.

Traders had been established on most of the Gilberts before the second world war but they had not survived the Japanese occupation. The only other non-Gilbertese there were missionaries. On many islands there were two Catholic nuns from Australia running schools and a French father. On the islands of Beru and Abaiang there were the main mission stations of the Protestants and the Catholics.

The choice of these islands as the bases for their missionary endeavours was not random. The first missionaries to arrive, well before the protecting power, had been Americans. They had established themselves on Abaiang, learnt Gilbertese, worked out a written language (unfortunately with only thirteen letters and no "s" although this is a common sound in Gilbertese) and compiled an English-Gilbertese dictionary. They converted most of the northern islands to Christianity and then set their sights on the south where, while keeping a station on Abaiang, they established themselves on Beru.

Beru was chosen as the Beruans had fought successful wars against most if not all of the other islands in the southern Gilberts. These islands had not been subjugated to a central power but the ruling clan of Beru had established its paramountcy on the vanquished lands and ruled them village to village in accordance with its beliefs and practices so that they became accepted as the political and social norms. (As a consequence of their success the Beruans became arrogant and inclined to idleness and the British Phosphate Commissioners refused to recruit their labour.)

The Protestant missionaries considered that if they set up their base in the southern Gilberts on Beru they would be taking on the pagan enemy in their stronghold.

When some years later Catholic missionaries arrived in the Gilberts they saw their problem to be converting Protestants to Catholics as much as converting pagans to Christianity. Accordingly they took their enemy by the throat, established themselves on the Protestant stronghold of Abaiang and also compiled a dictionary - French-Gilbertese. When the Bahais arrived they also established themselves on Abaiang so they could engage in a trial of strength against the stronghold of two colonising missions. However, they reckoned not on a third coloniser in the area - the British. The Bahais spoke loudly about how different Abaiang would be if it were under American rule, when everybody would have a telephone and a car. This appealed to some younger people on the island and when they drew up a petition for a change of sovereignty from Britain to the United States the head of the Bahai mission found himself served with a deportation order as an undesirable alien. He left the colony and his wife in a considerable hurry and the mission rather ran out of steam.

The rest-house on Beru was lonely and badly sited, standing on the west side of the island next to a large stretch of muddy sand, covered only at high tide by an inch or two of water, and on which it was no pleasure to walk.

Otherwise I only remember it by firstly eating nine crayfish in a day, middling sized and white, worried that if I did not consume them rapidly they would go off in the heat and secondly by confirming a case in the island court where a Protestant and a Catholic had inflicted extensive damage on each other after an argument about the rights and wrongs of Martin Luther. A rather stale cause for near mortal combat.

On Abaiang the rest house was vast, built on the scale of a maneaba. It was at least 25 feet high with partitions rather than walls dividing the space. It was placed well back from the eastern beach, almost in the middle of the land, and was the haunt of coconut crabs and rats. The crabs are to be treated with respect as amputating a thumb or finger with an enormous pincer is effortless, rapid and agonising, but the rats were enemies which I never managed to worst. They ate the soap in the shower, the wood of the food boxes and the labels of the tins inside so we had no idea what would appear on opening. They also ate green bananas and when Timeon thought we had put them out of reach by a rope they jumped three feet, wall to bunch, to continue their feast.

Catholic and Protestant missionaries in the Gilberts were generally on very bad terms, exacerbated as far as the men were concerned by differences in race. The Catholic fathers were Alsatian or Swiss and the Protestant pastors were British. Each sect only wished good for its own following and slighted the opposition at every chance. When one spiritual leader prayed for good crops in his half of a village the other half of the village of the opposing persuasion, unmentioned in the prayers, wished to start a war. In their newsletters school-boy or army like obscenities were flung at each other and the coarsest of allegations made. "The Awful Revelations of Maria Monk", concerning children born to nuns near a monastery in Canada, was published by the Protestants in an escalating campaign of abuse and in a form which implied the revelations were established historical fact and that Maria Monk would probably find herself in a familiar situation if she visited the Gilbert Islands. The Catholics in the "Star of the Gilberts" replied that the Protestants were only fit to eat the filth found on the western beaches." (i.e. the ordure under village lavatories). An offensive but not so effective reply was made by a Master of Arts of the other sect. For the Government it was difficult to steer a middle course. The Catholic bishop had co-operated without qualms with the Japanese during the war, not even raising an objection when New Zealand civilians were shot in cold blood, and he seemed delighted to cause the maximum inconvenience to the administration by reporting any supposed wrong to Rome from where it was relayed to London and back to the Western Pacific for righting. The Protestants made much of the religion of their monarch, the titular ruler of the Colony and certainly raised suspicions in the French Catholic hierarchy that they were in cahoots with the Anglo-Saxon rulers. They were, however, confounded when a Catholic administrative officer showed himself much more opposed to their mission than any good Anglican, nearly receiving one of the many excommunications the bishop dished out from time to time. Against this all touring officers held the Australian Catholic nuns, stationed in pairs on islands, in the highest regard and made a point of calling on them. They were delighted to speak to people in their own language, to hear news of the outside world and receive letters from home. In return they always dined and wined (communion variety) their visitors. My evenings with them were of the pleasantest. They were exceptionally kind and good women.

Apart from reviewing the Lands Court records and hearing appeals from the court's decision there were during my stay on Abaiang two field jobs I had to do. The first was to inspect a fish trap built, it was claimed, where it obstructed an older trap and the second to settle a disputed boundary to the Protestant mission. Travelling to the fish trap gave me pure pleasure. We chose an afternoon with a wind so blowing that we could sail on a reach and in two canoes, outriggers skimming the water, raced miles across the lagoon to islets on the western reef. There were three of them with a few palms, thin bush and silvery sand above turquoise water. The government canoe won the race and we stopped over the reef, jumped off and pushed our canoe to the beach. The beach sloped very gently to the lagoon and as we walked through the water we came upon wall after wall of fish traps made of coral and running out from the shore. Many had fish in them. Driven by our splashing, they shot rapidly to far walls or out of the trap and into the lagoon and freedom.

The magistrate, complainant and crew stopped on the dry sand and rolled cigarettes. I walked round the islet which took about 10 minutes.

There was nothing on it and because of the peace and isolation, hundreds of hours from civilisation, I would have much liked to spend a night on it and planned it, but sadly it never came to be.

The traps we had to inspect were equally old and at the right tide and season their owners each agreed caught enormous quantities of fish. If there was any obstruction of the complainant's trap it was ineffective. So the complainant lost his case and we raced back across the lagoon to arrive at the government station at sunset. I looked back for the islets on the horizon but they had gone, too far away to be seen, even with an old telescope in the magistrate's office.

As I walked home I had a flash back to Birmingham at dusk.

"Much better than Brum and paid to do it." A very smug thought.

In view of the land dispute affecting the Protestant mission I kept myself to myself for six weeks and spoke to or saw no European. The case decided I was asked and made a speech at the end of term ceremony at the Protestant school and went to dinner with Father O'Donnell at the Catholic station.

The Father had arrived in the Gilbert Islands that year. He was an Australian and English was his home language. He was broad-minded and tolerant and - until then an unknown practice - had even called on the Protestant Missionaries on Abaiang. When I arrived at his house he smiled and said, "Father R. is very pleased with your decision in the Protestant land dispute. I suspect he thinks it is a major victory for the Church."

We had a pleasant evening together and after talking over Christmas we decided he would come to my house and that as he would be saying mass at a distant church on Christmas Day we would, Continental style, have our big meal on Christmas Eve.

Two days before Christmas a ship arrived. Besides a fellow administrative officer and friend, George.B., it also carried two bottles of whiskey sent by friends on Tarawa. The whiskey was rather special being Johnny Walker Black Label. There was also some beer from the Wholesale Society and a note, "Herewith some Christmas cheer. We have debited your account for same." The beer I sent to Father and asked him to bring it cold and with ice from his refrigerator.

Off the land of Abaiang we made a passable meal on Christmas Eve. We sat at one end of the rest-house room with a pressure lamp over the dining table at the other end of the room. Bottles of Victoria Bitter lay in an enamel bowl filled with the ice Father O'Donnell had brought and more ice for our whiskey filled a thermos and an old sugar bowl. The Padre had my touring chair and George had his. My lot was an office chair with coconut string for the seat. Tinned nuts and to the disgust of the other two, dried raw fish, very smelly, constituted our appetizers.

We started our dinner with chicken soup and followed this with fish. A large mis-shaped piece of pork given to me by the Magistrate came next with tinned vegetables and some millionaire's salad from a coconut tree I had bought. The beer was well chilled and disappeared rapidly taking the coconut flavour of the pork with it. Thereafter, and probably wisely, as it contains an enzyme aiding digestion, we had pawpaw with coconut cream. Father O'Donnell then disappeared into the dark and returned with walnuts and sultanas he had been sent from Australia, and a bottle of communion wine. Timeon was sent to crack the nuts with a stone and we passed the wine round. The bottle was emptied and a certain haziness developed. We had coffee and the Black Label as a liqueur, two or three times. Then a beer to cool us off. The Father took off his clerical collar and his black shirt like a dickey. It rolled up from the bottom with a snap. George and I had a swing across the rafters. My hair was shorter than George's and I won on the strength of better vision. Our thirst seemed colossal and we got some more beer from the enamel bowl in which labels were floating freely and all the ice had disappeared. George insisted on cooling his feet in it. A religious argument started and George offered himself to the Father for conversion. Father said he was not ripe for it. George said his ripeness was full and complete. We both said this only applied to his feet among the beers. Father said it was twelve o'clock and Christmas Day and he could not drink any more. We pointed out this was only local Gilbertese time and in his home parish and the seat of his ecclesiastical superior, the Archbishop of Melbourne, it was only 10 o'clock. He had a drink. Soon after he said it was again midnight and Christmas Day. The time of the Catholic Church, we said, was most surely based on Rome. It was only late afternoon in Rome, practically aperitif time and many hours to Christmas Day. The double-doctor - of divinity and philosophy - accepted our logic and had a drink. At 4 o' clock we saw him to his lorry. George and I uprooted some bushes on our way back to the house and slept until lunch time. There was one beer left for us in a bowl of warm water. Also one of George's shoes.

5. THE SCENTS OF GHOSTS

Of all the rest-houses my favourite was on Tabiteuea. It stood on a rocky peninsula on the eastern reef without vegetation about it and without shade, in a constant wind. It was bleached a pale grey and the teba of the walls was dried and twisted, bending under the string which kept the sticks together. The rocks outside were covered with a film of salt, also grey, which in some places had thickened to a sparkling rime and as one walked out on the reef towards the sea it shook and trembled as waves broke upon it. In gullies waves rose and surged with fury against the rock, reaching up as if to flood the reef, then retreating in sullenness and disappointed gurgles to wait, rise and attack again. Behind on the reef in a secret invasion water welled and spurted from cracks and holes in succession and in diminishing strength as it sought to break the land from underneath and the rear. The battle was ceaseless and it was always a wonder that not only was the old rock standing firm but that the new rock - the live coral in the passages, gullies and crevices - was fighting an advancing and winning war as it slowly grew and feeding out of its enemy extended surely into the lashing waves.

A bay lay to the north of the house where long swells flowed in from the sea and there was surfing. The remains of a Gilbertese hut stood above the sand of this bay. In it had lived a man too old to go to sea and without a family to look after him. He had obtained his food by laying out lines in the bay at low tide anticipating that fish at high tide would take a hook. He lived well on catches, even having fish to dry and sell, but coming back one day when there was still water in the bay with fish in hand he had been attacked by a barracuda and although he had run, the barracuda, far faster, had circled and repeatedly dashed at his legs. In less than 16 inches of water it had taken bites out of his calves and he had to crawl up the beach where he bled to death before he could get to his house. No Gilbertese would live near the house but I chose a site for a new secondary school close by and like to think the boys of the school enjoy the swimming and surfing.

Tabiteuea is a long, nearly straight atoll with the largest single piece of land in the north. Many small islands are in the middle and another largish piece of land in the south. There is a reef in the north with a clear passage and a safe landing for ships' boats bringing in stores or taking out copra but the middle and the south of the island are a jumble of reefs and coral banks which make it very difficult for any sea going ship to get near enough to the land to

71

unload or load cargo. The South was some forty miles from the government station and landing area and the part of the Gilberts the most out of the grasp of the government, traders and missionaries.

The people of Tabiteuea generally and particularly in the south were regarded as pagan, this in the view of most members of Her Majesty's Colonial Service being an admirable state. They kept to old customs and ways, villages having their own traditions and engaging in inter-village rivalries which often led to fights. There were more murders on the island, usually over women, than any other island, adulterous wives were liable, according to tradition, to have their noses bitten off and girls danced bare-breasted at feasts. In honour of a visiting High Commissioner a village staged a dance which was condemned by Roman Catholic priest and Protestant pastor as immoral and indecent and although the High Commissioner appeared to enjoy it (while saying he had seen "much stronger stuff" in the Gold Coast), excommunications and removals from church of the organisers followed his visit, the offending organisers happily joining the Seventh Day Adventists. The neighbouring village preserved the last double decker canoe, 50 feet or so long, used for inter-island voyages and had the bones, some 250 years old, of the village's founder hanging in a basket covered with a turtle shell in the maneaba. When an old man dreamt it should be done, the basket was taken down, the bones washed and oiled and, in a ceremony at which the entire village was present, put into a new basket and lifted 10 feet above the ground by a new rope.

To add to the interest of the people and the island my first court case was held there. Two men, usually friends, had been given, illegally, methylated spirit. They had both drunk it, one taking his pint neat and the second taking his with 8 pints of water and then one challenged the other "To show he was a man" - i.e. to have a fight. The challengee had got hold of a knife to which the challenger had given counter by taking down a spear called a bakabota from the rafters of his hut, the bakabota's peculiarity being that it has sting ray spines lashed in a crown around its sharp end. The spines are poisonous and segmented so that they break easily into pieces. The men were too drunk to fight effectively but the bakabota did its damage with 7 spines in whole or in part embedded in the chest of the challengee. In due course he died and there had to be a trial presided over jointly by the Island Magistrate and a legal officer who has to be "one of Her Britannic Majesty's Deputy Commissioners for the Western Pacific", in this case myself. Present at the trial were also some 22 Island Councillors who acted as jury.

After 3 days in the island court during which time I had to write down everything said in evidence with frequent breaks while consulting my Cambridge law notes and trying to explain to the prosecuting policeman how his case should be conducted, we found the man guilty. Sentencing was reserved for the Island Council - no input from myself - and they gave the murderer ten years.

The prosecuting policeman was pleased and the island gaoler marched the convict out of court and off to gaol. Or so I thought. But bicycling up to the rest-house in the evening I saw him outside the kitchen talking to Timeon. He had a bush knife in one hand and a large jelly fish in the other. Both he and Timeon greeted me with flashing smiles and Timeon explained that the murderer was to work for him and was explaining how to prepare a Tabiteuean delicacy for my supper. Curiosity overcoming nervousness I went up to investigate. My main course was to be jelly fish but it had to be filleted and on Timeon's command with a couple of dashing strokes of the knife in front of my nose the murderer cut out blue circles in the middle of the jelly fish and indicated this was my food.

He thereafter arrived early every morning by bicycle. He parked the bicycle, found Timeon and they stood outside in the sun smoking Timeon's cigarettes. Five minutes later an elderly puffing warder would also bicycle up. Taking his time he would park his bicycle, recover his breath, join the smokers and take the prisoner's cigarette off him. When he spotted me coming out of the house he would put out his cigarette, take a baton out of his belt, turn his back on me and shout "Prisoner atten-shun".

The prisoner stepped forward and stood arms down, stomach out, face up with eyes screwed almost tight. The warder walked round him, straightened his lavalava marked with war department broad arrows and then marched up to me, stamped his foot with a force that would have bruised me for a week and shouted:

"Prisoner present and ready for inspection. Sir."

I looked the prisoner over, said "Very good. Warder. Carry on, please" - although carry on what I was not sure - and told Timeon to give the warder some metal polish so he and the prisoner could polish their belt buckles. Thereafter I went off to work, the prisoner was instructed in household duties by Timeon and in raking gravel by the warder. From the rate it disappeared they obviously all ate my food for lunch but compensation usually came in the shape of fish - hopefully bonita - for supper the next day.

One night there was a dance in a village to which I had been asked. Coming home late leaving the Government Station, a strong sweet almost sickly smell blew on me. I recognised it immediately - it was the smell of the flowers the girls had worn in their hair at the dance, a mixture of frangipani and a wild bush called mai. I stopped my bicycle and shone my torch about to see who was there. The beam lit the gravel of the compound, the trunks of coconut trees and a pandanus bush solid and slightly sinister in the dark with its leaves bent in the middle and hanging tangled. There was nobody around and thinking that the smell must have drifted across from the maneaba where the dance had been I bicycled on across the island. Nearer the east coast a breeze blew and thinking of the smell it seemed to me it must have been coming from the north. Odd, I thought, and went to sleep.

The following day at the Government compound I got off my bicycle and looked casually around for a frangipani or mai bush but there was nothing. Nor, thinking that a girl might have been walking from the dance, was there a path or, if she had been meeting a man, an acceptably comfortable place to tryst. There was also no vestige of scent.

At the end of the week the prisoner was told he had to come fishing with me. We did rather well and were both bicycling back to the rest-house with big fish when, at exactly the same place, the smell struck me again. I stopped and so, more slowly, did the prisoner.

"Is there a dance?"

"No."

"Are there girls going to a dance?"

"Where does that smell come from? A bush?"

"There are no bushes. I do not know where the smell comes from. I can smell nothing."

"Not the smell of mai?"

"No."

"Well, bring your bicycle here and you will smell mai and frangipani."

He moved nearer to me.

"Now can you smell it?"

Rather sulkily, he said "No, I smell nothing."

"There is nothing here that I can smell but I smelt this smell when there was a dance in the maneaba and I was coming home. What is it?"

"Please, you must ask the warder" and he got on his bicycle and rode off quickly.

At the house the prisoner in a hurry left his fish and bicycled away to the gaol.

The next day, coming home early in the afternoon, I spoke to the warder. Seeing us together the prisoner went off to the small hut in the compound that served as a kitchen and raked gravel out of sight and noisily.

I told the warder what had happened and he became half excited and half embarrassed. He produced a stick of tobacco from his belt and called to Timeon for a knife.

"Let me tell the Commissioner a story." Slowly he peeled the tobacco, sticky with molasses, and spaced out the peelings into a length of leaf. The story was obviously going to be slow, long and important so I sat. The warder continued his cigarette making and when he had finished offered me the brown untidy cylinder. It looked as lethal as I knew it to be from one previous smoke so I thanked him and said no. He put the stick of tobacco and the roll of leaf back into his belt, borrowed a match off Timeon and, lighting the cigarette, sat on a stone and talked.

His grandfather Ten Tematike, he said, had been an important man on the island when the British made the Colony. He had worked in a store owned by a white man called Turboti situated outside the village of Eita and on the lagoon. He learnt English and counting and was trusted by Turboti and all the people of Eita.

One day he heard in the store that there was a strange ship at sea. He went outside and there, beyond the reef, beyond the lagoon, there was a long grey ship with three smoking chimneys and at the front and the back short sticks coming out of little metal houses. There had never been a ship like that before off Tabiteuea and he went inside the shop and told Turboti and Turboti came out and said it was a British fighting ship and he told my grandfather, Ten Tematike, that they should go out on the canoe and see what they wanted. So they put the canoe on the water and shut the shop and sailed across the lagoon.

When they got to the ship they put down the sail and paddled close to it and my grandfather looked up and saw white people looking at them from the ship. There were more white people than he thought there were anywhere, more than brown people in Eita, so many that the ship was like a village but he looked hard and could not see any women or children and he thought that was strange. How could they have a village without any women or children and he asked Turboti and Turboti said the ship was only to fight and women and children would get in the way.

Then Turboti shouted at the ship and somebody shouted back and they threw some ropes over the side with pieces of wood attached to them and Turboti told my grandfather to paddle close to the ship and he did that and Turboti caught the ropes and wood and climbed up to the ship and my grandfather was surprised as Turboti never climbed a tree even to cut toddy. My grandfather sat on the canoe and waited and after a long time he saw Turboti on the ship waving his arm and he paddled up to the ship and Turboti got on the canoe and they sailed back to the land.

And when they got to the land Turboti sent a message to all the old men of Eita and said they must go the maneaba quickly as he had an important message from the ship. Not all the old men came. Ten Nataua was not there nor Te Natiera or Te Tibiana but there were enough. When they were all seated in their places Turboti asked if he could speak in the maneaba as he had important news to give and the old men said he could.

So he stood up and told the people he had been to the ship which was like a big village and had many white people who lived on it and the ship belonged to the Queen of England and the Queen had decided she must help the people of the Gilbert Islands because they had bad rulers like Tem Binoka of Abemama and suffered from people who came in ships and took Gilbertese away and they were never seen again. So the Queen was going to be the ruler of all the islands of Tungaru and at the next time when the moon was full her fighting ship would come back to Tabiteuea and it would bring the man the Queen had told to bring peace to the islands for her and he would come on the land and talk to all the people on the island and tell them about the wishes of the Queen and her rules. And when the fighting ship came back it would make a big noise, louder than any noise they had ever heard and all the people were to be ready to meet the man who had been sent by the Queen when he came ashore.

Then Turboti said and so that you will know this noise I will go out of the maneaba for a short time and make a sign to the ship and you will hear what the noise is like. So Turboti went outside and waved his arm at the ship and there was a loud noise from the ship, louder than we had ever heard and some smoke and all the people said they would know the noise again and there were many questions to Turboti but he did not answer them and said we should wait for the man to come from the Queen and spread the news to all the island. And he told my grandfather Ten Tematike that when the man from the Queen came, he was to help change the man's English into Gilbertese as the Queen's man would not be able to speak Gilbertese.

And it happened as Turboti said it would. At the next full moon the ship came back and Turboti and my grandfather went out to meet it and the ship made a big noise and Turboti got into a boat with an engine in it that steamed and hissed and came through the passage in the reef with the man from the Queen and about ten other white men with guns and he took them to the maneaba at Eita and all the old men of Eita were there and many other old men from all over Tabiteuea, and Turboti and my grandfather, Ten Tematike, put the words of the Queen's man into Gilbertese and told them the English were to rule all the islands of the Gilberts and would protect the islands with their fighting ships. He said he would come back to Tabiteuea in two or three months and live on the island and visit all the villages and tell the people what they must do to please the Queen.

Then he left the maneaba and spoke to Turboti and gave Turboti money to build a house for him when he came back and told Turboti to find a place where he could make cloth houses for the fifteen policemen he would bring with him.

And it all happened as the first Komitina said it would and his name was Biribi and he took my grandfather with him wherever he went on Tabiteuea and my grandfather taught him our language and spoke for Biribi until he could speak for himself. And when he left the island my grandfather, Ten Tematike, was made the magistrate of the island and ruled the island for Biribi and the Queen.

But my grandfather could only take small cases in the Court as he did not know the rules of the Queen well and had not had enough teaching from Biribi so when Ten Ratieta was killed by Te Tebao, the lover of Ratieta's wife, Nei Eritabeta, he locked up Tebao in the new gaol and sent a message to Biribi in Tarawa telling him of the matter and Biribi came quickly to Tabiteuea and brought some men from Tarawa who were his new policemen and they stayed on Tabiteuea and had to be fed by my grandfather, Ten Tematike, and they paid also money to Turboti for food from his store. And the Commissioner, Biribi, held a court in the new house that my grandfather had built and called some old men to help him in the Court and they all agreed that Te Tebao had done wrong in loving Ratieta's wife and wrong in killing Ratieta and they agreed again that Tebao should die.

The people all thought that the court had decided well and they agreed that Tebao should die and they thought that he would be killed by the guns of the Commissioner. But Biribi said no, it was not the law of the Queen that the man should be killed with guns but rather that he should hang by his neck from a rope until he died. When the people heard this they were shocked for it seemed that Tebao would be strangled and die a cruel death and my grandfather went to the commissioner and told him this and the commissioner said no, he would not be strangled as the commissioner would see that he fell with the rope tied round his neck and his neck would break and he would die quickly. And the people were satisfied when they heard this and said the Queen's way of killing people was good and they would come to watch the killing.

So Biribi talked to Turboti and borrowed some wood from him and he also talked to my grandfather, Ten Tematike, and he bought a big pandanus pole and they built a flat place with the wood with a door in it and the pandanus pole stood above the door and when it was finished they brought Te Tebao there from the gaol where he had been locked. And it took a long time for Tebao to walk from the gaol as there were chains around his feet so many people saw him walking with the Tarawa policemen behind him and the people also came to follow and slowly, like a very old man, he came to the place of the platform and Biribi was standing there and waiting.

The platform was taller than a man and there was only a small ladder to reach to it and Tebao could not climb it in his chains so a policeman carried him and when he got to the top he fell and lay like a sack on the platform. But he could use his hands so he crawled to the pole and stood and then Biribi told the police to put a chain round his hands and a rope round his body tight and a cloth over his eyes tight and when they had done all this Tebao found it difficult to stand and they had to hold him so he did not fall. And Tebao knew not what was happening and thought he was to be killed so he called "See, I die like a man" and the people watching also did not know when he was to die and a great sigh came from them and the brother of Tebao was Ten Amerika and he called out "You die like a man, it is true". But his time was not come for they had to tie a rope around his neck which hung from the pandanus pole and they did this and Biribi told Ten Tematike to ask

Tebao if he had anything to say but Tebao said only again "I die like a man" but this time there was no sigh from the people and Biribi then said "Pull" and a policeman by the platform pulled a long piece of wood and Tebao fell and we could see him under the platform and the rope went tight up through the platform to the pole and we knew that he was dead. Then Biribi told my grandfather that the police must take the rope and the chains off him and give his body to his family and this they did and he was taken to sea by his brother, wrapped in a mat as is our custom and put below the waves.

The gaoler paused and said nothing but took his tobacco out and made another cigarette.

But the platform of the killing remained and it was behind the office near the path to this house and that night as the dark was falling a policeman was walking along the path with a fish in a basket for the Commissioner Biribi and he heard a woman singing. He stopped and looked and there by the platform was Nei Eritabeta who had been the wife of Ratieta and the lover of Tebao. And she was dressed for the dance with flowers in her hair and a belt of woven leaves across her groin and she was oiled and beautiful and she finished her song and then she danced and the policeman did not like it and he went back to his house with the fish he had for the Commissioner and told the people what he had seen. And the people were silent and they said that Nei Eritabeta must have had a great love for Tebao and they respected that as then they knew it was not just lust that had brought them together but a great affection. So they left Nei Eritabeta alone but they heard her every night that week singing by the platform and saw her dancing.

Then the platform was taken down and the wood was taken back by Turboti and the following day the body of Nei Eritabeta was found under a palm where the platform had been and it was dressed only in flowers and the belt of fibre that our women used to wear. And soon after that Biribi sat in his office one day and talked to my grandfather, Ten Tematike, and then he wrote down in a book that nobody was to blame for the death of Nei Eritabeta and that the matter was finished.

But a year later a message came to my grandfather that Biribi was coming back to Tabiteuea and he came to this house to see that it was clean for Biribi. He looked in all the house and the kitchen and it was all as it should have been and then he left to return to the Government Station and, as he came near, it was almost dark and he smelt the smell of mai.

And he looked for a young girl and called out but he saw nobody and he heard nobody and then he knew he had been near the spirit of Nei Eritabeta for the spirits of our dead come back to this world as scents. And he met Nei Eritabeta many times after and my father and his brother met the spirit and I have met the spirit and my three brothers and the commissioners who come to Tabiteuea if they walk on the path in the evening also meet the spirit but nobody else on the island has smelt it, not even the family of Nei Eritabeta or the family of Te Ratieta. He paused and I thought.

"Do you think she is happy in her world or does she want to come back here?"

The warder looked taken aback and I wondered if I had offended him. "The scent is sweet." He emphasized "sweet".

"If she were not happy because she had been wicked the smell would be bad as of a rotting bird."

It was my ignorance of the world of ghosts that had surprised him.

6. THE MAUREEN

The boats that travelled round the Gilbert and Ellice Islands were few and far between and a touring administrator had to take whatever came along. When Timeon and I left Tabiteuea the ship that called was the Maureen and she was on her way to the Ellice Islands.

I knew the Maureen but had not travelled on her. She was one of a number of boats built for the short inter-island voyages of the Solomons, where land is never out of sight and seas are sheltered. "Surplus to requirements" she had on the orders of the High Commissioner been sold to the Gilberts to balance a deficit in the budget of the Solomons. But Gilbertese waters were very different to the Solomons and in the long swells of the open Pacific she rolled like a barrel, even weighted in her hold with 13 tons of ballast, and all who travelled on her and knew of the High Commissioner's chicanery in robbing our Colony to pay another spoke, sote voce, and not so sote voce, ill of the great man.

The Maureen had a speed of 5 knots so as she was going to Funafuti, some 400 miles to the south, and then back to Tarawa, 700 miles from Funafuti, we would be on board for at least 10 days.

The Maureen arrived and anchored. Timeon and I said our farewells and left sticks of dark brown sticky tobacco for the Magistrate and his staff and bottles of bright green scent "Evening in Hong Kong" for wives and daughters. The Magistrate came to the ship with us on the government canoe along with the prison warder, a policeman and the convict.

Over half the length of the Maureen was flat deck only 3 or 4 feet above sea.

Over the deck was a canvas awning suspended tightly from a small fo'c'sle in the bow to the bridge superstructure at the rear. As we came alongside a large cheerful Ellice islander put one foot over the ship's side, leaned out and said:

"Wait for the swell, I will give you a hand." He did so and I hurtled up and over on to the deck, kicked a fat black pig, which squealed, and nearly fell. A friendly shout came from the crowd of passengers sitting and lying on the hatch covers. The Magistrate was the next to be rocketed up. Then there was a pause while the canoe dropped on the swell. The sea came up, the Ellice Islander's hand went out and quickly the warder and the murderer arrived. Timeon and my clerk threw one piece of luggage before the canoe went down, and when it came up more luggage and the Government money box arrived, followed on the next swell by Timeon and the clerk. The Magistrate and I shook hands. He went back on the canoe and I went off to look for the Captain and a cabin.

The captain was Dick O'Caominh, strongly Irish, known as Paddy, and whom of course I knew. He had been master of a large ship who had come to the Gilberts on marrying and wanting shorter voyages and more time at home. When he had been shown the Maureen as his command he had commented she was about the size of a lifeboat on his last ship and refused to believe that she could be used anywhere except on a lagoon. Told that he had in three days to take her on an inter-island "shake-down" voyage he had disappeared to the club and after disposing of a large quantity of beer announced that he was going to see the Resident Commissioner and tell him he was leaving the Colony immediately. Both proved impossible. The Resident Commissioner had "too heavy a schedule" to grant him an interview until 10 days time and there was no boat from Tarawa to the outside world for 6 weeks. His wife pointed out that he would have to refund all their transport expenses should they resign. Totting it all up he decided to accept his command. On his first voyage a whale shark at least as long as the Maureen swam underneath his boat scratching its back on the keel. The boat rolled nearly 45° but recovered itself. Dick decided it was lucky and that he would stay with her. He made a great success of his job pencilling in on his Admiralty charts the correct positions of islands and taking soundings of the passages between reefs. He welcomed me to his ship and showed me his cabin which he said was also the chartroom, wheelhouse, sick bay, dining saloon first class, lounge first class and veranda cafe. The only bit of the cabin that he could call his own was an unscreened bed along a wall.

"Your cabin" he said "is by the engine room companion way. "And what else is that used as?" I asked. "The engineer's spares - now outside that door, left and first left. If you want fresh air use the boat deck," and he pointed up some stairs.

One night in the cabin was more than enough. It was a dark cubicle 6 feet long and 6 feet high fitted with two narrow bunks, one above the other and only inches apart. On the opposite wall to the bunks were greased spares for the engine which clanked and rattled and above the top bunk was a port hole which let in the noise of the diesel thumping loud and clear together with warm fumes which settled on the pillows and superfluous blankets. The ship rolled steadily, travelling across the swell setting from the east, and I felt myself as a spirit level tipped one way and then the other with the bubble in the liquid going down to my stomach and up again, not quite into the open air and then back down.

In the morning, thick-headed and queasy, I got out of my damp sheet and limped next door to the shower cupboard. Standing on a greasy duck-board and holding a pipe I tried to wash. As the ship rolled hot water came out of the shower head in short bursts and with my free hand and a cloth I did what I could to get clean. My limping foot started to sting and lifting it up I saw a bright pink strip where there should have been off-white thickish leather. Instantly from gossip heard I knew what had happened. A cockroach had eaten the sole in the night, unfelt and unseen. Omnivores three to four inches long they inhabited all the colony ships, sometimes in such numbers that a ship had to be anchored, deserted by its crew and sealed and fumigated. It would be weeks before my skin would be hard enough to walk bare foot on a reef.

Paddy offered me eggs and bacon for breakfast and sympathy for my foot.

"You must sleep with your socks on." This advice remained but not the breakfast. I was not quick enough to the ship's rail and vomited partially on the deck. Apologising to Paddy he replied:

"Don't worry, now Tessy will clean it up."

"Who's Tessy?"

"Sure Tessy's the pig. The one you put your boot to when you boarded yesterday. She's a fine animal and she doesn't mind a bit of bacon."

I told Paddy I would sleep on the upper deck.

"Sure" he said "you can have the dog box but you'll need a nail in the canvas. You won't mind a few fowls then now?"

"Do they scratch about on deck?"

"No, in a coop. You're best to have a look before you decide."

I looked and decided. The dog box was another coffin but of a spacious cut. Top, bottom, ends and one side were wood, the other side canvas, loose in one place from its nails. The box was lashed to the starboard railings of the deck and the chickens, fat Rhode Island Reds were in a coop lashed to the port railings. They seemed entirely unconcerned by the rolling of the ship and I imagined they thought they were happily living in the branches of a somewhat turbulent tree. However, my imagination was wrong. The chickens were not content with their lot and two escaped one day at feeding time. They ran around the deck pursued by the cook, jumped on to the wooden rail and when capture seemed imminent took wing and flew for an island with very real trees some miles away over the stern. The cook ran down the ladder to the wheel house. A loud shout came up which said something uncomplimentary about heathens and Paddy turned his boat in pursuit. He was losing the race when the birds tired and crashed into the sea a quarter of a mile away and far short of the trees. Seeing our approach they swam towards us making a pretty but incongruous sight, plump and brown on the heaving blue. Fifty yards from them we reversed engines and stopped, the cook and the big Ellice islander who had hauled us on to the ship dived overboard followed by myself. The two crew swam for the birds while I paddled around somewhat apprehensively looking into the sea and wondering what went on two miles below.

A second adventure for the chickens later in the voyage did not end so happily.

Usually at night they went to sleep and with only a few clucks and scuffles kept quiet to dawn. But one night a cockerel in the crate started to crow. After a quarter of an hour or so I tried shouting at it but this had no effect and every few minutes as sleep was about to deaden me it crowed loud and long. Eventually, staggering out of bed, I called the deck-hand on watch and went rapidly back to the box. The canvas was lifted up and a face leaned over me.

"Get rid of that hen that crows. Tell the cook what you have done in the morning."

The sailor went to the crate and squatted outside. The cockerel crowed. The sailor opened the lid and to a frantic flapping grabbed the bird and took it away and I thought "Good" and waited for sleep. Two minutes later a crow, prolonged and triumphant, woke me. Again I staggered from the box on to the deck and shouted for the deck-hand. He re-appeared, watched the crate, heard a bird, grabbed in the gloom and again left, protesting fowl in hand. Peace was established and sleep arrived.

Shortly after first light a loud and angry shout in thick Irish awoke me. The voice came through the deck and called the cook with uncomplimentary references to the colour of his skin, his lack of religion, the colour of his soul and his tarnished ancestry. "Luckily" I thought, "He won't understand a word of that."

I heard the cook's voice and some more Irish English involving chickens.

The cook said he didn't know anything about chickens.

Paddy yelled "Those chickens there. Shivering on the butter and crapping on the fish."

I understood. They were looking into the freezer. The chickens had gone in alive.

When the cook came up the ladder to my deck birds in hand a minute later, I was sound asleep. But the chickens gave no more trouble.

The dog box became my home. There was just room enough to sit up and write the touring diary when we had visited an island and I had rushed ashore to inspect records and meet the magistrate and island council. There was plenty of air blowing round the torn canvas and when a squall hit the boat there was a pleasant feeling of excitement combined with security as the rain lashed and rattled against the wood while I lay comfortably an inch away holding the canvas tight and keeping dry. The first day at sea I had got up for lunch and also for supper but the soggy mass of rice, fish, fresh but badly cooked, and tough wild chicken soon drove me back and the box also became my dining saloon, the sole menu being ships biscuits and water. With nostalgia I remembered the discussions on cures for sea-sickness we had had on the liner coming out to Australia. "Gin" voted one school of devotees. "Champagne" voted another school. The seas we met never really tested the cures but by common consent gin won before lunch and champagne before dinner. Either would have been ambrosial on the Maureen.

Paddy was paid a victualling allowance for each passenger he carried and the less they ate the more went into his pocket. Although he was it seemed not mean, he was concerned neither about the food he consumed - although he talked much of the curry his precious new wife would cook on his return to Tarawa - nor about the food for his passengers lying flat on the hatch covers of the main deck, where, suffering the same menu that I had endured but with the addition of raw onions, they vomited copiously. The smell added to my nausea and helped to keep me box-bound. To the pig it added competition and excitement as it patrolled the scuppers devouring what it could before it was washed away by the sea.

After a few days on the boat, however, it appeared that Paddy's navigation might be planned to augment his income from unspent victualling allowances. When we came to an atoll he would take the boat into the rough water at the north end of the island and then down the east side and into the rough water at the south end of the island. Taking the ends of the island was to increase his fish catch from the lines over the stern, but taking the eastern weather-side where there was no fishing advantage over the western side was calculated to keep us flat on our backs and away from food. It was no consolation that coral atolls were at their most romantic when seen a short way off the weather reef. Long blue breakers broke in white before the sandy beaches. A brilliant green band of bush marked the top of the beach and above them palms swayed in the wind and tossed their fronds. All the romance in the Pacific would have been happily foregone for an hour or two's calm water on the lee side. Rolled around in a box, mobile only on one foot, with a headache, constipation and a prison diet - I wondered somewhat savagely whether, if he had ever been on Maureen, the Resident Commissioner would have rescinded the reprimand issued to a ship's captain for "criticising government". The captain had been in Suva for repairs to his ship and on return to Tarawa had announced to all and sundry in the club that he had had the unfortunate experience of seeing the Maureen launched. "So green was the wood that I could hear the birds singing in the branches."

On the ship only Paddy was happy. He greeted me with joy whenever I appeared briefly below, told the joke of the chickens in the refrigerator - one more up to Maureen in his estimation - commented on the sea sickness of the deck passengers and asked if I had seen the weight Tessy was putting on.

One day the big Ellice Islander who had hauled us on board and rescued the swimming chickens came to see me. His name was Uriam (William) and he was the super-cargo on the boat. As such his chief duty was to see to the loading and unloading of cargo but he also combined the duties of first, second and third mate (or first, second and third officer on grander ships), chief steward for the deck passengers, bo'sun, coxswain of the ships boat, liaison officer and interpreter for the captain. He was interesting to talk to but alarmingly I found he could not take sights and knew nothing of navigation. If Paddy fell sick this meant there was nobody on the boat who could guide us across the sea and find an island let alone return us to the civilisation of Tarawa. Even more alarmingly there was only one engineer on board, Titivalu, a thin cheerful part Fijian who had a cabin off the engine room and never appeared on deck. If, I thought, Titivalu and the engine went wrong at the same time we would drift and nothing would help us. At least if Paddy were out of action we might by luck reach land. Uriam agreed with me but thought I was being morbid.

Uriam had a scarred and puckered thigh and I asked the clerk on his next visit to my deck what had happened to him. He looked taken aback.

"You have never heard of Uriam before. Sir?"

"No" I said.

"Nothing about his history?"

"No, nothing".

So the clerk sat crossed legged on deck and told me as I lay in the dog box the story of Uriam.

Uriam was the son of Tupua, the London Missionary Society pastor on the island of Vaitupu. Religion was in the family for Tupua was the great grandson of Leupena who had been the chief priest of Vaitupu when the last human sacrifice had been made on the island and the victim eaten.

As the son of the pastor Uriam had had a very strict up-bringing and was well educated and as a young man he had been appointed magistrate of Vaitupu. He had done outstandingly well in this post but one Sunday afternoon was discovered copulating with the pastor's wife on a pew in church. The news of this happening was over the island in a flash and almost before Uriam could adjust his attire a crowd had assembled outside the church and became increasingly angry. Uriam feared for his safety and ran to the gaol. Here he locked himself into the only secure building on the island for 24 hours until tempers had cooled and it was safe for him to come out. However, he had to leave the island and look for work on Tarawa. He soon got a job on a ship but he was not happy away from his people and wanted to return to Vaitupu. But the John Williams, the ship of the London Missionary Society, came to Vaitupu and the missionaries and church council of Vaitupu had a big meeting to talk about what should be done with Uriam and they agreed he should not come back to Vaitupu to live for 5 years. And when Uriam heard this he was very sad and also angry as the punishment was harsh.

Then the ship on which Uriam was working called at Vaitupu to load copra and the people of the island gave a dance to celebrate the coming of the ship and the money they had got for the copra. Uriam of course heard about the dance and he went to it and everybody was happy and did not mind his joining the dance. By late in the evening the dancing was fast and all the people were laughing and excited and Uriam was enjoying himself as he had not done for two years. Then came the last dance before he had to be back on the ship and it was a dance for the men and as Uriam danced and turned round quickly on the floor he held the top of his lavalava and when he faced the women's side of the maneaba he parted his lavalava very quickly and exposed his manhood to the women. And the women held their hands over their mouths and laughed and as Uriam danced faster, the faster he showed himself and the more the women laughed but he knew he would be in trouble and he left the dance and went back to his ship - this ship the Maureen - before the dance finished. And the next day all the island heard about Uriam's dancing and the women were ashamed and the Pastor preached against Uriam on Sunday and the church council met and agreed they did not want him back on the island until he was an old man which would be in ten years. So he travels on the Maureen and he gets off if the ship calls at Vaitupu but as soon as the copra is loaded he is back on the ship and he is always sad. He has 4 more years to wait until he can live on Vaitupu again.

"And the scar on his leg" I asked. "It looks like a bite."

"It is a bite, a shark's bite. Uriam was spearfishing in the lagoon when he caught a good fish, a parrot fish I think, and a shark came and tried to take the fish and Uriam would not let him have it which he should have done and the shark bit him on the leg. But he is not frightened and he is a good fisherman."

"Does he still spear fish?"

"Oh yes, he still spears fish."

So the next time Uriam came up to the deck we talked about fishing from which I gained much knowledge of the islands and the difficulties of their inhabitants' life.

Over the centuries, before Europeans came to the Gilbert Islands, the Gilbertese had developed skills and customs that enabled them to thrive in an environment as unfriendly to large mammals as a hot desert. On these flat sandy islands rising not more that 6 feet above the sea the first comers found no water and no vegetable food. They had to dig wells and pits for tubers. The digging was often through coral rock and the hardest tool available was the shell of a giant clam. When they found water it was brack and moved up and down in a well with the rise and fall of the tide. Vast as the Pacific is, it was for centuries travelled by humans paddling canoes, sometimes as much as 2,000 miles between start and destination. The Polynesians spread themselves from Hawaii to New Zealand and to islands in a belt 3,000 miles wide across the southern Pacific. Their voyages, culture and language are the best known and studied but there are people like those who inhabit Nauru and Rotuma who are found only on single tiny islands and whose language is spoken nowhere else. Their history is a mystery except that it is probably right to surmise that they came from the north or north west.

The Gilbertese also came from the north but in what numbers we do not know. If they left some of their race behind when they moved the language has been lost to them. They had a system of navigation, using the stars at night and possibly locating land from wave patterns by day but why they settled at the islands they came to inhabit with their harsh drought stricken climate and infertile soil we do not know.

Perhaps they found people before them and lived with them or were rejected by people living on islands where life was easier.

Whatever, the Gilbertese or their predecessors had to bring coconuts with them and may have had to bring pandanus palms. The pandanus was vital to survival in times of drought for the fruit can be made into various heavy and sweet puddings which will keep for years. A thoroughly nasty fruit to most people's taste it was nevertheless so important to the Gilbertese that they have over 300 names for it, distinguishing minute differences in appearance and taste much as in Europe there are numerous names for the many parts of a church or types of motor car. For coconuts which not only give up bearing early in a drought but cannot be made into long lasting food there were only 7 names, distinguishing the stages in the nut's growth. In their colonising voyages the Gilbertese also brought the only mammal that could survive on the island - the Pacific rat.

As the Gilbertese filled their islands with people they developed a culture in which the ownership of land played an enormously important part. Individuals fought individuals, villages fought villages and neighbouring villages became so hostile that to go from one village to another was to look for death. Clans were formed as were alliances large and small, all with the aim of subjugating neighbours and dispossessing them of their land and even one island in the Ellice Islands was conquered, a remarkable long range naval and military operation as the island, Niutao, lies 300 miles from the nearest island in the Gilberts. In war, as in fishing, building, digging, canoe building and everyday life the Gilbertese made the best use of the few materials their environment offered. Body armour and shields were made from woven coconut fibre, helmets from the thick spiny skin of porcupine fish and swords from coconut wood with shark's teeth neatly sewn into grooves.

European technology, religion and disease altered or destroyed the old ways of life. Metals made all work easier, religion brought writing and books while introduced disease, particularly measles and tuberculosis, killed hundreds if not thousands. Such a killer was measles that the British quarantined completely any island where an outbreak occurred and let nobody out, the diseased population having to cope on its own as best as it could. Strict religion led to laws being enacted on some islands ordaining silence in the evening for prayers and making Colony wide some fornications or adulteries a criminal offence - although a Gilbertese would usually only lay a complaint if the sexual offence was against the teaching of his old religion as well as against Christianity.

Dried coconut and copra was exported, bars established, at least 13 Europeans murdered for molesting Gilbertese wives and the local whale population wiped out. Pigs, cats and dogs ("kameas" - come heres) were imported and if they did not like fish and coconut they were fed on imported food while imported food changed the importance of the pandanus palm and of land - although the peace declared by the British left many land claims which were in the process of being settled by battle as unresolved and a source of much work for future lands commissioners.

The Gilbertese had glitches in adapting to the ideas and practices of the new order but in their main economic activity, fishing, they found the new materials nothing but helpful. New fibres and plastic took the place of coconut fibre rolled into string on women's thighs, metal hooks took the place of wooden hooks and sharp metal knives - the most useful of all European tools - took the place of clubs. The only fishing technique which did not become easier was the operation of fish traps. Owning two lines of stones on the reef formed into a V and encrusted solid with shells and corals remained as easy and as efficient a way of collecting fish as it always had been. A good trap could take a ton of fish in one tide and the owner's only problem remained that of getting the fish ashore in the few hours before the next tide was high enough to let the fish escape. With such an amount of fish dried he had no need to work for another year.

If waiting for fish to fill a trap was the minimum extreme of effort and danger then catching black marlin was, in my eyes at least, the maximum extreme of effort and involved danger which, as luck would have it, never came my way. A hooked marlin will at some stage when it is being played, jump from the sea, perhaps more than once, so the catch is identified. Should the fish be brought too close to a canoe it will charge and at 50 - 60 miles per hour, weighing half a ton and with a sharp hard spike on its nose, it is definitely in the super-rhinoceros class of projectile. Canoe and fisherman will be pulverised. To avoid this one of the two fisherman in the canoe awaits the moment when the fish is thirty feet or so from the canoe and near the surface of the sea. Armed with a knife he will enter the water and at one or two miles per hour swim towards the marlin. The fish does not recognise the danger of such an awkward slow moving, almost drifting, object and with even less brain than a rhinoceros waits in the water, puzzled and hurt by the cord entering its mouth and digging something sharp into its jaw. The fisherman dives, plunges his knife into the back of the fish's head, the marlin is paralysed and the fisherman, like a stiff bow legged frog, swims up to the surface and back to his canoe. At 7d or 9d a pound for the flesh he would have become rich by his morning's work.

7. FLYING FISH

I learnt much about fishing from talking to Uriam on the Maureen as it slowly rolled and thudded island to island in the southern Gilberts and larger Ellice. But he not only talked but acted.

At one island we fished close to the reef for castor oil fish. Our line was 200 fathoms, nearly 1300 ft. long and the letting down and hauling up of such a lengthy cord seemed hardly worth while for the sake of a fish whose flesh was oily and could be poisonous. I said as much to Uriam.

"Tomorrow night we will do something exciting."

"Catch a shark?" I asked "or a barracuda?"

Uriam said no. Only big sharks are exciting - three fathoms long or more - and as we won't troll we won't catch a barracuda.

The capture of the large and fast appealed to me.

"No? What then?"

"Flying fish."

"But you can't get them with a line" and (thinking of someone I had heard of in the New Hebrides who used a shot gun) "We haven't a gun."

"We use nets, Sir, at night." He paused "What is this about shooting them?" So I explained and countered "What is this about nets at night? I have never seen any net except a throw net used in shallow water."

"We shall see tomorrow."

The following evening we stood at the top of the beach watching the light wane. To our right the Maureen rolled at its anchorage and my mind was torn between talking to the magistrate and thinking how pleasant it was to be off the boat and missing supper.

We got the Government canoe out of its shed and down to the reef. A prisoner brought long flares of coconut fronds bound in pairs. They were laid in the canoe except for one that the Magistrate lit and stuck vertically in the stern. Above our heads it smouldered - a red warning beacon and at eight feet high well out of the way of spray.

We pushed the canoe out making for a break in the white foam along the fringe of the reef that marked a gully. Two of us got in waist deep, a man held the bow and the prisoner the stern keeping us head in to the swell.

"Go" shouted the bow man and hauled himself into the canoe. We paddled hard and the outgoing water took us at speed, we juddered on the lip of the gully and then fell into its maw with water pouring both sides from the higher reef. Fast as we could we went into the ocean surmounting the incoming wave, down its back and on to almost flat sea. We stopped.

I looked behind me. There was no prisoner.

"No," said the Magistrate, "he did not get on. There he is in the passage", and among the white water pouring off the edges of the reef a black ball of a head, often submerged, came towards us.

The experience had been sudden and dramatic - leaving the secure land where all was settled and ordered, down a constricting turbulent half tunnel and suddenly into the formless sea limitless in depth and range. This vision of a birth was jumbled in my imagination with the picture of the mariner of "infinite resource and sagacity" being swallowed by the whale in "How the whale got its throat" from the "Just So Stories" - the mariner swimming hard on a torrent of water pouring down the black whale's throat and escaping the perils of the sea into a safe extensive interior.

The prisoner's head moved slowly towards us, a comet-like trail of phosphorescence stretching behind. He reached the canoe and while we leant on the outrigger scrambled in from the other side. We took up our paddles and set off for the south of the island leaving the lights of the Maureen behind us.

Flying fish are found in all tropical waters. There are a number of different species varying from 4 ins. to 20 ins. in length and they are surface fish feeding on minute animal and vegetable matter. At night they come close to land but can only be caught in numbers when it is moonless.

We paddled twenty or thirty yards off the reef. Here the ocean bottom or, viewed differently the top of the land, was close below us. Long swells passed in stealth and silence beneath the canoe, then marshalled into waves and, secrecy cast aside, burst violently and noisily on the reef to our left.

Above the battle line of sea and coral stood the island's palms in a tall black wall, the tops of the trees still and crenellated against a paler sky. Near the bottom of the wall yellow lights shone slits and loopholes and I imagined people safe in their castle watching the attacking hordes of the sea hurling themselves on the outer defence of the reef but always being broken and retreating in chaos, the cry of their charge muted to the weak gurgles of death. But the sea was persistent. For the same water, broken and white on the reef, ran off to the ocean, to rest and re-order before rising again to hurl itself on to the coral. If the waves caught our canoe they would grind it remorselessly into fragments just as 100 years before they had caught the Lawless and killed it on the reef at the village the Gilbertese now called "Roreti".

In front of us, perhaps three hundred yards away, a line of gold suddenly glittered in the dark.

"They fish" said the magistrate and I realised the flares of the fishermen we were to join had been lit. As their canoes were formed in a line parallel to the reef and we were looking along the line, the flames of the burning leaves formed a narrow band of colour which descended slowly as the flares burnt down and lowered the flames towards the sea. On the fronts of the canoes figures swirled and stretched, leaning out and bending back, rising and twisting in a display of unco-ordinated gymnastics, their gyrations accompanied by laughter and talk.

The lights died and as we neared them the canoes turned and paddled towards us, line ahead. We blamed our prisoner for making us late and when four canoes had passed and turned we also turned and faced the land. The smouldering flare from the stern of the boat was passed to the bow man who stood up, balancing on the gunwales and picked up a long handled net from the outrigger as he did so.

"Ready?" somebody called.

"Yes" from all canoes and our man on the bows loosened the binding at the top of the flare.

"Light" and he swished the flare down and up. Crackling flames broke out from our flare and the flares on the other canoes. For a second or perhaps two there was nothing except light on the sea. Then the waters spouted fish and the air filled with fish. They rose from the pool of light which circled the front of the canoe, thrashing the sea with their tails, gained height, opened out their fins and with a last flick of their tails sped into the darkness behind us. From our front, fish hurtled out of the gloom into the light and, if they were lucky, past us and into the dark. There was no flapping of fins to keep them airborne. Their pectorals extended out wide and rigid and the only

94

movement, apart from flight, was if the body banked slightly in its path, one fin and flank going up a degree or two and the other fin and flank going down a degree or two. Otherwise their course was straight and level.

As the fish came out of the dark into light and back to dark, their colour changed as rapidly as their speed. Briefly grey, white, silver they became gold and glistening with beady black eyes before they changed silver, white, grey and invisible. So many rigid bodies hurtled at speed past us that it was easy to imagine that one was inside a very large atom and that the fish were whizzing electrons on gigantic circuits of an invisible nucleus.

It was the fish that landed short and lay motionless that became our catch. The man with the net swung left and right extending or shortening the pole in his hands and dropping the net over a fish in the sea. The net was then swung over the canoe and with a quick twist the fish disengaged and dropped into the hull. Some of the fish that fell into the sea jumped up rapidly and flew out of the light but most floated still, looking dead, and made easy catches.

The scene was so entrancing that it was not until a glossy curve of water appeared before us that I realised we had been moving slowly forward and were looking at a wave rising, curved like a snake, to strike the reef. The net man doused his flare by sliding up a binding and sat down. The canoes turned in line to the north and we paddled away. As our canoe had been at the south end of the line we had had the worst station since we had been nearest to the previous area fished.

Now it was our turn to have the best station furthest from the previous fishing areas so we paddled past the other canoes and became the leading canoe in the line. Somebody behind us shouted and as disciplined as a naval force we stopped, turned to face the land and at a second shout lit our flares.

We worked our way northwards, fishing station to fishing station, with our lights driving the flying fish out of the sea between the canoes and the reef. It was a succession of robberies. The fish all taken at one station, we turned and canoe following canoe passed through the night chattering to each other and banging and splashing our paddles as we approached the next site for an exhibition of plundering skills and ardour. We stopped, turned and lit and in the light of the flares the net men bent, twisted, stood, squatted and swung as fast as they could as they took the booty from the sea. Behind the net men were the paddlers, two or three, their skins fading from gold when they were closest to the light to natural brown at the back of the canoe, shadow and light flickering over them from the waving flames of the torches or, coming off the sea, reflected rippling across them as they paddled slowly across the looted water. With my white skin incongruous in the yellows, brown and dark purples I felt very out of place, although accepted by all the crews as one of their party who was happily in on the raiding.

But we were not the only thieves of the night. Splashes sounded from behind us and somebody said "Te urua", a fish I never saw and for which I never found the English name. One station later a heavier fish splashed "Bakoa" (shark). He had taken an urua, and then a fish 5 to 6 feet long, broad in the jaw and tapering to the tail slid under the lighted surface of the sea.

"A big one" said the Magistrate with authority. This was disappointing as "big" for a shark would for me have been at least 10 feet. It was enough though to be exciting and I sat very still, giving up any idea I had of standing on the canoe and trying my skill with the net, and hoped that the wood between the shark and the canoe, only 3/8 in. thick, would keep us safe. About our feet the dying flying fish were beating against the canoe making a noise that must have been very audible to the shark with a clear indication of where his next meal could be found. My father's story of tying up a bleating goat as bait for a tiger came unpleasantly to mind.

But the shark did not seem interested in us. He chased the urua and the urua chased the flying fish.

At the edge of the northernmost light we could make out the grey bodies of the fish travelling in all directions and the plops of their landings came from behind us and among us.

"They are too frightened. No more fishing tonight" said the net men and we said our good nights.

Uriam asked me about our fishing and I told him how much I had enjoyed it.

"Did you use the net?"

"No. A shark stopped me" I explained.

"Yes, it is skilled. You must practice." He thought. "You must also learn how to catch fish with a noose."

"I am not a cowboy" and I had to explain about cowboys. Uriam found it difficult never having seen even on a film a cow, horse or a wide open space and, cowboys not being in the Bible, he thought I was storytelling but then I did not believe him fully about catching fish with a noose.

It was early morning and another island without a lagoon, and we were paddling just beyond the reef with the sun so low that we were in the shade of the island's palms. The tide was out and on the reef, separated from each other by a decent distance, people squatted clearing their bowels before the day's activities. A progression of shouts marked our passage. The squatters heard all about the Commissioner and the fishing and we heard all about village matters, the well stocked store now that a ship had come and the ease or otherwise of bowel movements, with accompanying comparisons and agreements.

Above the beach cooking smoke lay as a mist under the palms and we saw the church and pastor's house, the pastor himself large and dressed in white, looking at his world from the top of the beach, and the first children of the day at school, to whom I was of great interest.

Our fisherman was at the back of the canoe and in his mouth he held the end of a fishing line. The line was short and hookless and dragged in the sea a piece of fish tied to where the hook should have been. In a leaf basket on the outrigger he had some small fish and a short piece of wood while on the outrigger itself was a tapered pole with a line at the thin end and a gutted fish attached to the line.

We reached the north of the island and the open ocean. The swell became stronger and as the canoe started to roll and pitch a great unhappiness rose in my stomach. When we came level to the last beach we lost the shelter of the land and as we rounded the end of the island and headed north-east the sight to the front struck me with unease and foreboding.

The dominant swell was as always from the east but here, beyond the northern beach, swells also came from the west and north. Far out to sea the waves formed in lines and like disciplined regiments of cavalry advanced steadfastly on the land. They gained in strength and speed as they approached the beaches and rose high in shallow water and with an air of menace and invincible power sped to a charge, spray flying like the hair of helmet and mane, and curled forward to sabre sand and rocks. But over the gentle shallowing beach they reached too far and lost cohesion and purpose. Crossing waters tumbled and fell into a churning confusion of green, blue and white creased with red glints from the reflected sun. Bewildered eddies, not knowing where to run, fled unscathed out to sea or were ridden down by an incoming wave. Some with a remnant of discipline and a remembrance of their orders carried on towards the shore and died by the guns of cutting

97

rocks or the fragmenting blasts of coral boulders. A few reached the softness of the sand where they whirled and disappeared without trace. It was a self inflicted and confused defeat and hewn stones which had once stood on the water's edge and now were high up the beach measured the decisiveness of the land's victory.

We left the worst of the broken water and entered on long sloping valleys of smooth sea. Suddenly the fisherman hissed. "Te boara (kingfish). My bait is gone."

Rapidly he hauled in his line and standing, feet on gunwales and facing sternwards, he took up the pole and cast out the gutted fish. We back paddled and brought the canoe to a stop. The paddler in front of me turned and put his finger across his lips, then his mouth to my ear.

"Don't knock the canoe."

The fish tied to the pole had been so filleted that there remained only its head and two strips of skin. In a wide circle the fisherman trailed it from one side of the canoe round the stern to the other. Then he reversed direction and quite suddenly a fish 4 feet long, striped vertically in blue and white and shaped like an enlarged mackerel, appeared behind. Then as suddenly as in a conjuring act it disappeared. The fisherman stopped circling the bait and, putting the end of the pole in the water, thrashed the sea making a spray. Then he lifted the pole, dragged the bait again and for a second the kingfish re-appeared.

My paddler in front whispered.

"The kingfish is very angry."

The fisherman waved his hand at us and slowly we paddled the canoe forwards. He put the pole and its bait on the outrigger, picked a fish out of the basket and started to chew, spitting out morsels into the sea. The kingfish appeared, disappeared and appeared again, taking two pieces of chewed fish. Still spitting the fisherman picked up the short piece of wood from his basket and a length of line. He looped the line over the ends of the wood, and spitting out a piece of fish, set the noose about it, a foot under the surface with the bait at its centre. As the canoe moved forward he paid out line letting the noose remain stationary. The kingfish came back, following the trail of fish, and unhesitatingly, entered the noose to take the bait. The fisherman's arm leapt up. The noose tightened, slipped along the body to be stopped by the tail, and within a minute we had the kingfish in the canoe, clubbed and still.

The catch made was fast and clean and I started to say so but the paddler in front indicated silence and whispered "We may catch more".

So my questions had to be stored.

We took two more fish and then I could ask "Why fish like this?"

The fisherman explained. "Kingfish swim in shoals. If a fish is caught on a hook its thrashing frightens the other fish and they would swim away. There is no pain for a fish caught on a noose and it is taken out of the water so quickly that also there is no time to frighten other fish." He paused, "It is time to go. We haven't been lucky today."

We paddled again through the war zone and back towards the government landing. It became my worst memory of the Gilbert Islands. I felt seasick without being able to vomit, the plank seat became harder and harder, my hand blistered and the crew did not paddle together. All on one side and then all on the other and although I tried to paddle on the opposite side to the rest it did little good and we veered on a zig-zag path. The sun was hot and the breezeless air oppressive, making me irritable, tired and wretched. Luckily nobody could see my face and I hope I was not rude to my hosts. I think not, for we saw a sole fisherman paddling his canoe with a shark as long as the canoe across the outrigger and hull.

"He is a lucky man" I said. "He fishes for an hour or two and catches enough food for 6 months. I wish I were a Gilbertese fisherman." This was a complete lie at that moment but they laughed at the joke.

I finished my work on the island and returned to the Maureen with half a kingfish to share. My section was eaten soused and raw. It was delicious, better than tuna, and a treat unfortunately never repeated.

We had left the waters of the Gilberts and were travelling through the Ellice Islands to Funafuti, the capital. At day break on the second day the ship was moving without rolling and it seemed we must be in the lee of an island so I got up and found we were off the passage to the Funafuti lagoon. Surprisingly we were motoring in large circles not attempting the entrance nor drifting to save fuel. I went down to the Captain's cabin. Tessa, black, fat, dirty and smelly lay in the bunk. Paddy was at the helm keeping the ship on its curve and talking to the pig.

"'Tis a greedy old woman you are." Tessa grunted.

"You've gone and got yerself a blockage now." For me he added, "There have been too many not eating in the last day or two."

I asked when we were going into the lagoon and was told "We cannot gain it now. The set's eleven knots and Maureen can only make seven. It'll be two hours yet."

The passages outside lagoons are famous fishing places, so I said: "Stop the engines and I will catch you some lunch."

Paddy was most indignant. "Stop the engines indeed. Then the boat will be all over the place and what'll Tessa make of that?"

At slack water we went in and landed at the village on the far side of the lagoon. Paddy put down two anchors and left Uriam in charge. "It's only half an hour I'll be" and had himself rowed ashore. Earlier than his half hour he was back with a large bottle of castor oil and I was ashore myself. Six hours later at high tide and slack water we left. A crowd of guitar playing, weeping, beflowered Polynesians gathered in canoes to say farewell, leaving a crowd of young men on the boat who shouted at them as we up-anchored. We made the passage and were out to sea with Funafuti a smudge on the horizon. In groups of two and three the men jumped off shouted "Tofa" (goodbye) and started to swim to the island.

"Sharks?" I asked Uriam.

He laughed. "No. They will all make it but they will keep away from the passage."

Tessa was out of the bunk and back on her deck. I was off the deck and back to my box.

We stopped at an island on our way back to Tarawa - and Uriam caught a shark fishing off the boat. He opened it up. The sole item in its stomach was the leg bone of a pig that had been thrown over-board, fleshless, three days before.

We were both impressed and agreed sharks were a problem that needed investigation.

The author (far left) with a ray

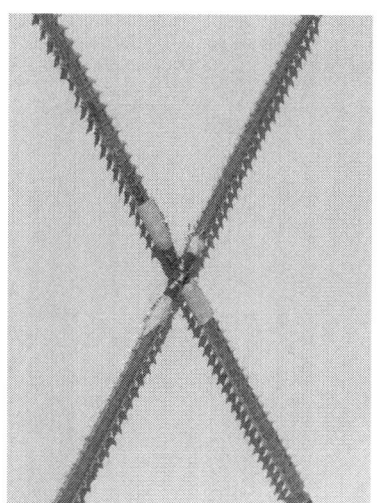

Shark tooth swords

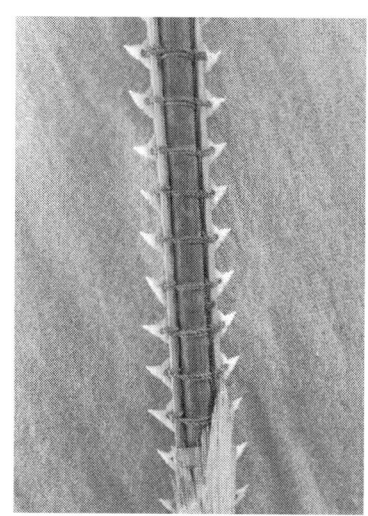

Detail of sword

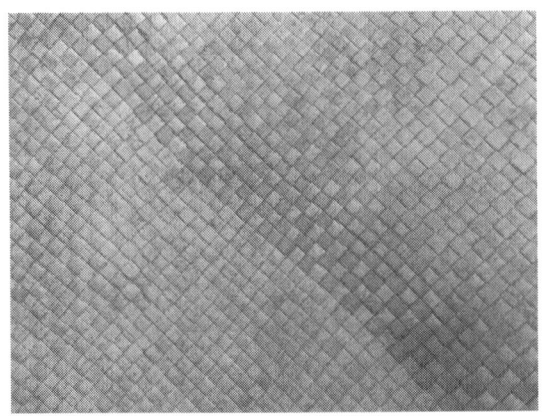

Hand-woven Gilbertese mat

Coconut cup

Model canoe with outrigger

8. HUNTING SHARKS

My boyhood reading had included many stories of tropical seas. Without fail sharks were omnipresent in the "warm waters of lagoons".

"Triangular fins" "cut" surfaces and "great grey shapes" hovered beneath them. Any fish or animal, especially man, coming within distance of the monsters was dashed upon and devoured in a "welter of blood-stained foam".

Less lurid but no less dramatic evidence was provided verbally by Australians on the liner by which I had travelled from England. At their beaches a watch is kept by volunteers on towers for sharks. If one is sighted bells are rung and to avoid attack you must make pell-mell at top swimming speed for the shore. The river at Brisbane was full of sharks which fed on immigrants who wrongly believed they would not enter fresh water, while statistics were quoted concerning shark attacks and the savagery and determination with which these were made.

A favourite tale concerned a shark which before the 1939 - 45 war had been caught at sea and put in an aquarium in Sydney. It was not a large fish, perhaps 4 or 5 feet long but after a few hours in the aquarium it vomited, producing a large part of human leg.

The newspapers and the police were most impressed. Extensive inquiries were made for missing persons and the public urged to report suspicions. The leg was removed from the shark tank and a reconstruction published of the person of whom it had formed part. The shark was also removed from the tank, killed and dissected to see what other human parts it might contain. There was nothing. But on land next to the area in which it had been caught inquiries said to be "penetrating" were made and a search instituted. From the Sydney underworld rumours flooded up and eventually the eaten man was identified. It was established he had been murdered but nobody was arrested. Thereafter the affair rather fizzled out. The Sydney underworld had its reputation little affected but the newspapers in articles and correspondence which lasted for months took up sharks and greatly enhanced their bad character. Nobody had any sympathy whatsoever for the shark which had set the whole furore in motion and which from a rather different point of view had had its efforts in keeping open waters clean rewarded by capture and murder.

The only book found in the Gilberts for identifying fish was the "Sea Fisheries of Southern Africa". This excellent work by the late Professor J.L.B. Smith of Rhodes University describes the tropical fish which extend to the warm waters off the coasts of Natal and Mozambique. Many if not most of the same fish are found in the equatorial waters of the Pacific. I read in the book about selected sharks as follows:

Tiger Shark (Galeocerdo Cuvier)

"A voracious scavenger which eats almost anything, is one of the most fierce and dangerous of all creatures, not easily frightened and pursues its prey to the shallowest water. A large specimen has been stated to cut a man in half with a single bite."

Hammerhead Shark (Sphyria Zygaena)

"Large hammerheads are most ferocious and fearless and do not hesitate to attack boats. Large specimens are among the most dreaded of all marine creatures."

Grey Nurse or Ragged Tooth Shark (Cacharias Taurus)

"Stationary in even only four feet of water the largest specimen is hardly visible against a sandy bottom. If an unwary bather approaches within reach there is a savage rush and usually another fatality. The jaws of a ten foot specimen would easily sever a human head or thigh."

Man Eater, Death Shark, Blue Pointer (Carcharodon Carcharias)

"Attains 40 feet and a weight of at least two tons.... this swift voracious and ferocious shark is a terror to all who venture on or in the water.... This shark will come close to boats and snap viciously at an arm overside.... A 12 ft. specimen can bite a man in two, a 20 foot specimen can swallow a man whole."

"An 18 ft. monster caught near the coast during a calm in a fog following heavy rains ashore was hooked and finally shot by the captain. Dragged aboard it was cut open and found to have in its stomach the foot of a native, half a small goat, 2 pumpkins, a wicker-covered scent bottle, 2 large fishes quite fresh, a small shark and unidentifiable oddments."

"Teeth 5 ins. long have been dredged from the depths, indicating sharks of 100 ft. with jaws at least 6 ft. across. These monsters may still live in deep water but it is better to believe them extinct. Such a shark could swallow an ox whole."

104

Professor Smith was himself a voracious fisherman hooking out of the water whatever he could. So in the Gilbert Islands was I to an extent. My extent being that while I was not happy about seeing the many different coloured and shaped fish of the lagoon and reef being extracted from their habitat and beating out their lives in suffocating air, catching tuna or marlin was "sporting" - I suppose an exercise in male machoism - while catching a shark would be not only "sporting" but ridding the sea of a danger that could but benefit the environment - sub-consciously I suppose benefit in particular the environment in relation to man. Sadly in retrospect this was not so and people of my youthful thinking have done extensive damage to shark populations all over the world, sometimes in the cruellest manner such as cutting off a living shark's fins (for sale to the bottomless pit of the Chinese market) and letting the shark free. Sharks are late breeders and top predators. Remove them from the sea, the unfit multiply and food chains are skewed.

There were no such thoughts or worries as we planned our shark fishing. Nataua, my clerk, told me that he had gone fishing with a District Commissioner and had easily caught sharks 4 fathoms long. Their fishing hooks had been attached to large floating drums and the lines to the drums secured to their boat by thick rubber cut from the inner tubes of lorry tyres. The sharks had towed the drums until exhausted, drowned - a shark has to swim to breathe - and then hauled to the side of their boat.

We could not find suitable drums or inner tubes so had to make other plans.

A friend in the club told me how he did it.

"I harpoon a devil fish then we cut it up and catch the sharks in the Tarawa passage. It never fails."

He produced the harpoon, 6 feet long with a head that swivelled. Small holes had been drilled through the head and shaft and a match inserted in the holes kept the head in position when the harpoon was thrown. The shaft of the harpoon was iron, about an inch in diameter.

"There is no way I can throw this" I said.

"Don't worry" said my friend "I can do that". I looked at him and decided that as he was about as broad as he was tall that he probably could "do that". On devil fish he was not very forthcoming except that they were black, large and could be easily harpooned on the surface of the lagoon, so I went back to Professor Smith.

He was not nearly as positive as he was about sharks.

"Family Mobulidae"

"Devilfish or Devilrays"

"2 genera are recognised"

"A. Mouth below head Mobula"

"B. Mouth at front of head Manta"

The good news was that they were "often" harpooned and usually tow boats for a long time until exhausted" or "for hours".

The bad news was that they were "quite mild creatures unless attacked", will "sometimes leap from the water, and has upset or swamped boats and killed men in this fashion", could have a weight of "over 2 tons", could be as wide as 24 feet and might or might not have a basal spine to its tail.

I knew something about ray spines from the trial I had taken at Tabiteuea and what people in the Gilberts had told me. One spine could be poisonous enough to kill very painfully while Smith wrote in regard to stingrays "The only hope of recovery (if stabbed) is rapid removal of the spine from the flesh and irrigation of the wound with some antidote. Even then many stab wounds prove fatal while those who recover often suffer for some time from general ill-health." A spine on a 2 ton fish would, I imagined, be of a fair size and lethality.

We set out on a Sunday morning early. Our boat was the tug belonging to the Wholesale Society and as it was used for towing it had a low stern without any protuberances on which a rope could catch. The small freeboard would make it easy to haul on board anything large we harpooned or caught. However, the boat was nothing like as long, 4 fathoms, as our potential prey. I asked what one did with sharks we caught longer than the boat.

"You tie them alongside."

"Doesn't that bring a lot of other sharks?" My thoughts being on the feeding frenzy in which a book had informed me sharks indulged - with a certain disdain:- "They feed on their own kind with the same ruthless avidity as they devour anything else in bloodied water." George, my friend with the harpoon, shrugged and laughed.

"Perhaps."

He did not seem concerned so I kept my imaginings to myself but thought that three or four fathom sharks might do a fair amount of damage to a bloodied boat, particularly if inspired by ruthless avidity. As our stern was only half a foot or so above the sea and of thin decking it would easily succumb to large bites. If a 2 ton ray which had ceased to be "mild" on being attacked jumped on to us the boat would be flooded and sunk - it was old ex-wartime, roily and creaky and the engine, taken from a jeep or the like, gave us no speed to escape a pursuing devil fish. If I were spared in such an attack I could swim to the nearest wrecked landing craft on the reef but if sharks were around I could see no possible escape. Mentally I also shrugged.

As soon as we had cleared the harbour and a buoy we turned towards the submerged reef on the west side of the lagoon. The tide was high and there we could find, George assured us, our basking rays.

He was entirely right. As we closed on the reef stationary fins perhaps 6 inches long, shaped like black triangles poked above the sea. They looked like the dorsal fins of sharks but when I said "Sharks" was told "No. Big rays. See that the fins are in pairs. Those are the tips of the wings."

The sea was smooth, like a cloth of dark velvet spread flat to the horizon. The enclosing reef of the lagoon was deep enough not to rumple it but shallow enough to show its presence by a lightening of colour.

It was in and along this swathe of pale water that the fins were placed. Most pairs were positioned to show that the bodies to which they belonged faced along the reef. Some of the fins waved slowly, breaking the smoothness of the sea and pushed small ripples away. Other fins suddenly disappeared without trace below the surface of the sea and others also without trace as suddenly appeared. There could only be, quite out of sight, an enormous quiescent herd of rays grazing in peace like antelope in long grass in an African game reserve with only the ends of ears showing, occasionally going up as heads were lifted or disappearing as heads were lowered. A scene on which we were entering, smellily, noisily and disturbingly, roaring and rattling as we fouled the air with fumes, bent on killing or maiming.

As we reached the reef we entered the herd and saw the bodies to which the fins belonged. They were black, shaped like large skates, some small with five to six feet between wing tips, others three times the size, fifteen feet tip to tip. Thin tapering tails were countered by wide mouths in thickened heads and two long black and white fins rounded at the ends and with an eye at their base, curving in front of the mouth. The fish hung in the water motionless, no longer a herd but squadrons of Vulcan bombers silent on an air-field.

107

Our boat reached the reef and we turned north cutting our speed and travelling slowly. The rays paid no attention to us and I wondered whether our ugly chugging could be heard by them. Even the spreading wake of the boat as it passed over the fins did not disturb them. Black and evil looking as they were their indifference was startling. George stood in the bow with his harpoon and faced forwards. His left hand he stretched out and signalled the helmsman. We altered course and he picked up the harpoon, balancing it like a spear, a rope from its rear end tied to a ring on the deck. Two smaller harpoons, also roped, were on deck by his feet.

The boat was travelling for the middle of a ray facing away from us. We went into neutral and cut the engine to an idle. Some ten feet in front of us the ray started to swim, undulations moving along its wing, its tail broke water and it went into a dive. Six feet from it George threw the harpoon. It holed the ray in the middle and would have passed clear through but George looped the rope round the bow post. The helmsman threw the gear into reverse and we lost all way. Taking a small harpoon George handed it to me. "Have you got your knife?" I had.

"Jump" he said.

As a child one of the great if not the greatest fears of my life was to pass from one carriage of a tram to another. Walking along a corridor with a parent in attendance with the scenery rushing past outside was exciting. The large windows let in light and there was a continuous change in scene even if it was only of black brick walls with an occasional advertisement as one passed through the inner suburbs of London. People young and old sat in the compartments reading or talking - the older of the old more interesting than others, with men dressed in Victorian or Edwardian fashions, spats, wing or stand-up collars, gloved, their hats on the luggage racks or knees or hanging on hooks.

Old ladies were not so interesting as they wore too much purple for my taste and fell into two categories, the buxom and heavy or the thin, vacant or ascetic and their clothes loose. Sometimes there were children with whom, if eye contact was made, an instant awareness could be reached. An awareness never widened or explored in our transient and noisily temporary world.

At the end of the corridor excitements vanished. As we reached the outside door, the corridor changed direction diagonally, we passed the door of the lavatory, grubby water leaking out under its bottom edge and we entered the dark gate of hell.

Our walls became corrugated and heaving. They extended and shortened, twisted and opened, canted and levelled. Black snakes of pipe hung in loops along them and the only light that came in was from chinks and gaps that also let in the smell of smoke and sometimes steam. If I held a hand I could manage in this connection as far as its middle but then I could go no further. Here two iron plates met. The one on which I stood was firm but the one in front, on which I had to step, was turning, moving towards one if the locomotive, I suppose, braked or we reached an incline and away if it accelerated or we came to a decline. Here there were always peep holes and the outside world of gravel and sleeper rushed past at horrifying blurred speed, and my great fear, completely irrational, came on me that somehow I would fall out of the train and on to the track. Otherwise the slow turns of the metal plates, underfoot, of one carriage on another would catch my feet and grind off a toe.

Depending on their patience or not a parent or aunt would try to coax me over, cajoling or ridiculing. Sometimes I would be lifted but usually I had to be given a hand and with shut eyes would then cross the Styx, scurry through Hades and enter the bright paradise of the next well lit corridor.

So it was as I stood contemplating the gap between the boat and the black back of the ray. I imagined myself leaving the agreeable sunny deck of the boat and leaping on to an animal from hell which could do only demons knew what. The tail of the ray was between the boat and its back and while there was no visible spine anything might be hidden underneath the tail. At the far end of the ray there was obviously an enormous mouth marked at each end by a flipper which could push you tight into a throat. There should not be any large teeth but it seemed obvious that the mouth could hold you and drown you or crush you much as a toothless frog crushes and breaks a hard cased insect.

"Hurry" shouted George "or it will pull itself off the harpoon."

"Where shall I cut?"

"The front of the wing. Stop it from swimming."

Well, I was braver than I had been some 20 years earlier so when I jumped I kept my eyes open - a streak of light from the inside white of a flipper flashed at me and I was over the centre of my corridor. I landed feet first on the fish, slithered on to my front and thrust my knife into the body.

109

The skin was not slippery but a little rough and I did not slide off as I thought I might have done. Holding the harpoon where it entered the fish I pulled myself forward and stabbed into the front of the wing with my knife. The wing waved and I was into the sea with a vast mouth like the open bonnet of a big car in front of me. At unbelievable speed I swam past the wing and round to the rear. Grabbing George's harpoon I pulled myself on to the back and, one hand on the shaft, stabbed again. There was a thump and George arrived on the island-like animal and we attacked ferociously.

But there was no battle. The ray lay inert and made no further flap.

Nor did it twist or turn or try to dive but quietly wallowed, bleeding brown into the sea, brutally assaulted by the two of us as we severed its muscles.

The crew threw us the two short harpoons and we pushed these through the back of the ray, then, sure it was disabled, we jumped off, swam to the stern of the tug, washed and clambered on board. We took the ropes of the harpoons and pulled the ray tail first to the back of the boat, killed it with an axe and hauled it on board. It spread across the deck, half of each wing hanging over the side into the sea. A very crashed Vulcan bomber.

The first part of our plan had gone much more easily than expected. Our devilfish had not swamped or towed us and we could identify it as Manta "Mouth at front of head" rather than Mobula "Mouth below head".

We had had intense excitement and effort in making the kill, the excitement heightened by the thought that sharks might be attracted and attack the ray with us on its back. Long minutes had become short minutes and I suppose we were again on the tug within a quarter of an hour of first choosing our victim. The sea was still dark and calm, a party of black noddies was still diving for fish on the far side of the reef and the twin fin tips of other rays were still popping up and down, hardly rippling the water. The scene was only different in that the pale sandy coloured after-deck was covered by our enormous holed and smashed, black, white-lined catch. Even in death it looked evil and at that time if not in retrospect I had no compunction about having killed it. Now, I thought, for its liver and our irresistible shark bait.

From the expression on their faces it was clear the three Gilbertese crew were not happy about the death of the fish. There were no volunteers to help butcher it and leaving the helmsman to himself the other two went to the bow and smoked in silence. George and I took the axe and knives and started to cut up the fish.

110

"What's the matter with them?"

George shrugged.

"Probably belong to the ray clan, I think. It is a big one."

If they did or one of them did it would, we knew, be against custom to kill the clan emblem. So we left them alone.

We motored along the reef, the sea darkening beneath us, towards a pole approximately north that marked the lagoon end of the deep water passage. Blue smoke from our exhaust hung in the air and very slightly and slowly we rolled gunwale in and gunwale out so that the sea flowed into the back of the boat and side to side where George and I were working.

Our knowledge of anatomy was completely lacking and it was only after a lot of probing and cutting that we located towards the back end of the ray a great bag of dark brown flesh encased in a glistening membrane. George pronounced it the liver. The size of it was impressive and assuming an ox and the ray were about the same weight it was much larger than anything that had come out of any ox that I had seen.

I was in a mess, spattered with fish and blood.

"I would like a quick swim."

George was horrified.

"No, you will be shark bait. All the blood has been going into the sea and anything large could be following us."

That rather put me off but I thought up a plan.

"Let's stop the launch and look for fins."

George was doubtful.

"A fish might be deep. You would not see it."

"Well, I will hang over the side and wash a bit at a time." George did not like that either but I did it - very quickly and on the qui vive.

We reached the pole and turned west into the middle of the passage. The engine was cut, we baited our hooks with a sandwich of ray's flesh with liver filler and lowered them on rope three to four fathoms into the sea. To make their presence known to all sharks in the area we squeezed out liver over the stern and threw the wrung out skin to left and to right.

"Now the big ones will come" said George.

The tide had started to ebb and we drifted through the passage. To make sure that small fish were not eating the bait we hauled up our lines for inspection. The bait was untouched but we took the liver off and replaced it. A hundred yards away a flock of noddies and terns squawked and fought above a feeding shoal of fish.

"Should we not go there?" I asked.

"No" said George "It is probably only tuna. We shall do better in the passage."

But we caught nothing and saw no fish and a mile out in the ocean past the last buoy we hauled in lines, started the engine and motored back to the lagoon, squeezing and throwing off liver as we went. Well into the lagoon we stopped the engine, let down hooks and drifted again with the tide into the passage.

It was nearly ten o' clock and getting hot. There was no wind and the engine stank of hot oil. The steering chains rattled and the slosh of bilge water as it went side to side made me feel queasy and George and I talked of the Betio club and a cold beer or two.

We threw out bait in small pieces which, attracting no visible fish, sank out of sight. Any sea creature at the bottom of the sea passage must have thought it was a strange day with food for the third time drifting almost continuously down from the bright heaven above.

Quicker on the stronger ebb of the tide we drifted through the passage and out to sea a second time. Not a bird or fish did we see.

As we returned through the passage to make a third run, the helmsman pointed. On the starboard side ten yards away was the fin of a shark. It was small, three or four inches above the water, and black. It was moving in the same direction as us and slightly towards us.

We reduced speed to keep pace with the fin and George and I threw bits of ray in front of it. We turned towards the shark so as to cut across its track. We threw small pieces of liver. We threw the baited hooks. The fins moved away from us and then disappeared. Our frustration and disappointment was intense. We talked over abandoning the run but decided not to.

Starting again from the lagoon side of the buoy we drifted. The liver was nearly finished and we threw out small pieces interspersed with large lumps

112

of flesh from the wings of the ray. In the middle of the passage one line tightened then the other. Dropping our knives George and I went to our lines. The helmsman was already pulling in George's.

"Small shark" he said.

I took my line and started to pull in. There was a steady drag on the end as if a lump of coral had been caught and broken off. No vibration or uneven tugging, which is the usual feel of a hooked fish, was present.

"George, have you got a fish?"

"Yes, a small one".

"I think I have a nigger head and have broken it off. The line's dead." "No, it's too deep. Probably a shark."

I continued to pull in. There was a dull thud. I turned. George was half way across the tug holding his line to pull his catch against the side of the tug. The helmsman was standing by with the axe. Behind the stern of the tug lay the grey body and darker tail fin of a shark.

"Hit it in the middle now. We will let it bleed into the sea."

The helmsman moved aft and struck with his axe.

"What is it?"

George spoke to the Gilbertese.

"Death shark."

From Professor Smith's book I remembered "Death shark, Man-eater, Blue-pointer .... swift voracious and ferocious will come close to a boat and snap viciously at an arm overside ...."

I continued to haul.

"Quick the axe."

I brought the shark alongside. The helmsman drove the axe into its head and then almost severed the body with a blow behind the dorsal fin. We roped both sharks round their tails and pulled them on board. With the small harpoons as levers we forced the mouths open and wrenched and cut the hooks out. We baited them again and dropped them into the sea.

The sharks we slashed and cut. We tied them so that their tails bent over the stern and their bodies bled in the sea. George assured us that next to ray's liver nothing was more certain to attract sharks than the blood of a shark.

It seemed as if he were right. No sooner was my line down than I caught another shark. It was hung over the stern with the other two.

The ray we cut up quickly and threw lumps out to both sides of the tug.

Behind us somebody sucked his teeth. George and I turned. The helmsman was pointing and standing up, we followed his finger.

"There it is. There it is." One of the crew called and jumped on to the middle of the roof over the motor room. George and I moved to the high part of the deck at the bow of the tug. I saw the shark. It was twenty five feet from the tug and looked about three feet under the water. Refractions of light would make it deeper and closer. The body was bulky and half as long as the tug. Streamlined and elegant, it was marked laterally from behind the gills slits to the thinnest part of the tail with equal stripes of dark brown and yellow.

"Tiger shark."

There was no movement in the body of the shark. Through the light green surface water it slid round and round. Neither closer nor further did it move. So constant was the radius of turn it could have been on a string tied to the centre of our boat.

On a plank six inches above the ground one can walk without fear. Depending on age and head for heights the same plank can be walked on without undue alarm at six feet above the ground. At one hundred feet there are few who would walk unconcernedly across. Put the plank over the cliff edge at St. Kilda twelve hundred feet above the sea and how many people in the world would walk ten feet to the end and back? If it were night and one did not know where one was there would be on the other hand no difficulty in the walk.

Commonplace thoughts but they came to my mind on sight of the shark. In our tug we had motored without fear on the lagoon and on the ocean. We had stopped and started the engine to drift in the passage and then travel back to the lagoon. We had jumped off the tug into the sea, killed a big fish and swum in the water without fear. In the passage and on the open ocean we had lain flat and washed our arms while cutting up the ray. Moving about the tug we had slipped and nearly fallen and done nothing more than laugh.

I fell into a reverie watching the shark pass round and round the tug.

I thought of us with a broken engine drifting across the Pacific followed by the shark and joined by others. I thought of the shark sliding towards somebody who had fallen into the sea leaving a pale brown cloud in which limbs and fragments of body would slowly gyrate. I thought of a shark three or four times as long swishing the tug with its tail.

A splash went up in front of the shark. The shark veered away. George pulled his hook and line back. The helmsman threw out some big lumps of ray. The shark ignored them and continued to circle the boat. A deckhand baited the second hook with liver sandwiching it between pieces of flesh cut from the small sharks we had caught. He swung the chain on the hook and landed it in front of the shark. Quickly the trace and bait sunk. The shark reached them in its orbit and swam over them obscuring our view until the bulge in its belly receded and they appeared behind the anal fin. Seemingly it paid no attention to either the splash or the trail of blood the liver and flesh had left in the water and through which it had swum. Even taking account of the short sight of fish it must have seen at least the line and more than probably the trace and bait.

Four times on each side of the tug the baited lines were thrown to the shark. On the hooks were fixed successively liver and flesh of ray and liver and flesh of shark. The last shark caught as the freshest was used and the bait slashed and stabbed to make it bleed freely in the water. After the move it had made from its path on the first splash the shark changed its course not in the slightest and took no notice of the meat, hooks and lines falling in the sea about it.

George coiled his line and laid it down on the deck out of the way. He picked up the big harpoon, made sure the head turned freely on its swivel and with a match fixed it in position. He came to the bows and put the harpoon down. He lay flat on the deck.

"Hold my legs, please."

"What are you going to do?"

"Tie the rope to the ring over the bows."

He pulled himself over the bow post. I held his ankles bracing my legs against the combing. He made his knot with the rope and got back on deck.

He picked up the harpoon and coiled the rope down near his feet. With legs apart and left hand holding the rope he waited. The shark came round on its circuit and George threw. The harpoon fell short. The shark swam on. George pulled the harpoon in. He had to put a fresh match in the head and after doing this got ready to throw again.

Anti-clockwise the shark came round. George threw. The front two- thirds of the shark disappeared. Foam covered the water. The tail broke surface and, bent over the sea, moved furiously. It disappeared. The whole shark came to the surface and as violently as a hooked minnow thrashed and wriggled. It rolled half over and a partly opened mouth appeared underneath. It dived. For a moment the rope went tight. Then slowly and slackly it sank into the water. The shark disappeared.

George started to pull the harpoon in. He laughed.

"A bad throw. I did not get him in the middle."

"I think the harpoon went right through."

"Yes." He laughed again as he pulled the harpoon on board. "Look, he has bent it."

Near the middle the harpoon had a twenty degree bend in it. Until straightened it was unusable.

An aura of anti-climax settled on us. Our object of excitement had vanished and nothing came to take its place in the sea, which, with the sun overhead and its rays passing direct into the water, had lost its glancing colours and turned leaden and inanimate. The birds which had dived and squabbled were no more, their varying noises being replaced by a listless and repetitive slapping of wavelets against a hull rolling slowly and wearily and supporting on its deck an ugly mess of mangled fish, pink body fluids, and broken carcases.

I looked away towards the land and was cheered.

The sand on the reef at the end of Betio shone the dazzling white I knew from my house, telling us the tide had dropped. Breaking the line of white in a vertical perspective were the black hulks of the wrecked American landing craft, which were also familiar. Further along there were houses among half grown trees and, in the air above them, the tall heads of the three full grown trees that had survived the war. Between Betio and Bairiki the stretch of sand separating the islets lost detail to become a shimmering grey over a line of light that was the ocean beyond. Past Bairiki on the east-west arm of Tarawa the land disappeared, marching into nothingness, to meet the equally invisible north-south arm of the atoll. Nearer us was an islet, Bikeman, an oasis of white and violent green, near the middle of the lagoon.

"At least we saw a shark worth talking about."

"We may get another soon. We will put the lines down."

As George spoke the deck-hand on the roof shouted: "There is one. There is one. Another tiger."

From the deck we could not see and we scrambled on to the top of the motor room.

As large as the first a second tiger shark had appeared. It was coming towards the tug from the ocean.

It was a little far to be seen except in outline and its movement through the water was slow. Only the tip of the dorsal fin showed and it was taking a path that would bring it near but not directly to the tug. It moved its head and neck from side to side. It reminded me of a dog snuffling on a scent.

We got the lines down and started to throw flesh from the ray and sharks into the sea. A little liver remained and this we kept as bait for a hook.

The shark came within ten feet of the boat in an oblique approach. The slightest of undulations moved through its body and the side of its mouth appeared upturned. It had a grey-white eye bulging slightly, like the eye of a cat with the iris full open. For the size of the shark the eye was small.

The shark passed by the lagoon side. Here it was up-tide from our drift and would not be able to taste the blood in the water. I thought it would leave us. More obviously than the first shark it had been following up our scent, and it might go if it lost it.

This was not so. The shark established itself in a circuit some twenty five feet from the tug. Somewhat more slowly than the first shark it moved again without visible movement round the tug, travelling anticlockwise.

We drew up and threw our lines into its path. We cut up ray and shark and the small remaining amount of liver and scattered them in the water.

"Two" grunted the helmsman and we saw a second shark in the same circuit as the first.

117

We transferred our efforts to catching the second shark. Then to both sharks. Splash after splash was made by falling lines and hooks and the water spattered with pieces of flesh. The sharks were supremely indifferent.

Rolling in my line I baited it with a large piece of fish. After forcing it round the curve of the hook I worked it as far up the chain as possible.

"Don't throw anything else into the water. Cut some big pieces of shark and put them over the side. George, don't throw your line for a minute, we may be frightening them."

He did as he was bidden and I let my line 50 feet down into the sea.

One shark continued to circle. The other disappeared.

"Gone home for lunch", said the helmsman.

My line started to move without a tug or a judder. I struck hard. There was no give. Coral? No, we were too far from the reef.

"Quick, I have got one."

George dropped his line and got on to my rope behind me. We pulled hard but gained nothing. The helmsman and a deck-hand got behind George. We worked the line to the stern so they would have room to pull. Slowly we hauled in.

There could only be the large shark on the line. If I had not been sure I would have said we had a large baulk of timber hooked. There was no vibration, no tugging, no hard sudden pulls. The line stayed almost vertical in the water. A large mass resisting movement by the awkwardness of its shape was the only possible catch that could be on the end. Steadily we hauled. A light patch without shape appeared in the water beneath. As we got it closer it took form and colour and turned into a shark. It was hooked at the side of its mouth and the steel chain came out taut just in front of an eye. It moved neither fin nor tail nor body. It neither snapped nor rolled nor jumped. It was a solid weight on the line and seemed already dead.

Many yellow fin tuna in the 50 to 80 lb. range have I caught. Also a few over this weight - the heaviest being 122 lbs. They were all caught for food and not in the way of sport. They were all caught trolling with a heavy line and hook which they would be unlikely to break once hooked. What a different experience! A tuna jumps and dives and beats so fast that the movements of his body cannot be followed. Even if he has been pulled some hours, hooked on an unwatched line at night, so that he is tired and almost drowned he

118

fights like a mad thing when brought in. With a boat stopped it takes two men to haul an 80 lb. fish in and then care has to be taken not to burn and cut one's hands on a running line. Likewise wahoo, marlin, sailfish all fight and struggle to death.

We got the shark alongside and pulled his head to the middle of the boat: "Hold him. I will get the axe."

Swinging the blade high I brought it down on the head just behind the cat-like eye. The blade glanced off and skidded along the shark. So unexpected was its turning that I nearly went over the shark into the sea. Twice more I brought the blade down on the head but not in the least did it cut into the flesh. Thin white lines on the skin were the only marks.

The three on the line were as dismayed as I. It seemed as if we would be left with a large, live, even if dormant, shark which at any moment might decide to make a fight or take a snap at the boat. Remembering the struggle the harpooned shark had made and the ease with which it had bent the iron bar in its body it seemed as if we might have some excitement.

"Try the middle" someone said and I moved down the shark to the dorsal fin. Raising the axe again I brought it down just behind the fin. It sunk in to about one third of the blade. A white cartilage was exposed in the shark marked in concentric rings. Two more blows and the "backbone" seemed severed.

Even these blows on its person brought no life to the shark. Supposedly the severing of its back-bone killed it but it was impossible to say "it is still alive" or "it is dead". Instead of being a large live deadly fish it might have been a lump of white meat on a fishmongers slab in England. Alive or not we took good care to keep away from its jaws.

The tooth of a tiger shark is distinctive. There is at the base a semicircle of white with a serrated edge. Growing out of the semicircle is a smooth projection like the canine tooth of a dog. It is set at a slant to the semi-circle and not quite at the top. With imagination the tooth looks like the humped back of a porpoise above the sea. The head and tail are in the water and the dorsal fin sticks up.

The tooth is a most efficient cutting device. The sharp point is to break and enter a bitten object and the curved serrated edge to cut it.

In the open mouth of the shark we could see a row of these teeth. A few were missing. Behind were five or six rows of teeth diminishing in size to the back of the mouth and lying flat on the roof of the mouth. Where a tooth was missing in the front cutting row, a tooth from the row behind had started on a turn through a right angle to replace the missing tooth.

In the air the dark brown stripes on the shark were narrower than they had appeared in the sea. When it was swimming round the tug the light of the sea rippled by the waves had made it look much like a tiger in pattern and colouring. Still and in the open air there was little similarity between the aquatic hunter and the hunter terrestrial.

We put a rope round the shark's tail and tied it with its head at the stern alongside the tug. With the two small harpoons we forced the hook out of its mouth. We started to fish again.

Luck was with my hook. Within five minutes we had caught in an equally unexciting fashion the second shark. We tied it up on the opposite side of the tug to the first shark and set off home.

As we came into the harbour at Betio there was great excitement. A large silent crowd of Gilbertese assembled and all small boys swimming in the water got out. The trail of blood from our launch, said George, could lead in other sharks from the reef.

A European turned up and unendingly took photographs. The two big sharks were removed from the water by a crane of the Wholesale Society. The larger measured 11ft. 2 ins. and weighed - after a few hours of dehydration in the sun on the wharf side - 588 lbs. The other was an inch or two shorter and a few pounds lighter.

The flesh of the sharks large and small soon disappeared into hungry bellies. The jaws of one I had cut out and attempted to dry near my house. Opened fully with the upper and lower jaws almost in a straight line a dried mouth with teeth standing up is an impressive ornament. However, my jaw seemed reluctant to dry properly and acted for a fortnight as an attraction to most of the flies on Betio. It was then buried with the idea that ants would eat the flesh away. But it disintegrated and all I have left is some of the teeth.

9. SOCIAL LIFE

My living had to be earned on one of two islets of Tarawa. One called Bairiki, the other Betio (Bay-she-o).

Bairiki was the seat of the Resident Commissioner and senior civil servants. It was small, shady and quiet with a neat village of Gilbertese and an assortment of government personnel all aware of their hierarchical ranking in terms of the official circular on precedence.

Betio was in almost every way the opposite. It was large, some two square miles, it was hot owing to the remains of an American airstrip down its middle and it was noisy with a shifting population of Gilbertese and the excitement and vices that go with ports and boats, besides having on its road a landrover, a car and two lorries. It was also divided in its loyalties. The District Commissioner was top of the Government pecking order but in terms of power the Manager of the Wholesale Society was pre-eminent, having under his command money, jobs, ships and a well stocked store. There were also, beholden to neither the Government nor the Wholesale Society for employment, independent traders and artisans.

Both islets had clubs which were the nuclei of communal social life. The Bairiki club was owned by the Government and had two sleep-outs where transients could stay as well as a tennis court. It was built like a Gilbertese maneaba, lofty, cool and rather solemn. The sole patrons were civil servants clothed white from shirt to shoes drinking in the evening with their peers, to many of whom they had spent the day writing letters, not all of which were amicable.

Apart from jokes against the Government - not when the Resident Commissioner was present - jokes were told against other civil servants and we talked about leave, laughed when the Assistant Marine Superintendent's dog bit through an electric flex and disappeared down the beach giving the most miserable howls, played liar dice and listened to the story of how the postmaster, after a good dinner with the Assistant Accountant-General, was shown slides. He mistook the Assistant Accountant-General's wife whose husband had photographed her naked on the beach for a teenage boy and said in a loud voice "There is young Jim Evans". Food for plenty of salty remarks.

The government storekeeper had a wife who had been on the stage. She wore ankle length dresses, usually pinkish, long gloves, straw hats with flowers and carried a parasol. A pleasant woman but she kept to herself except where her husband was concerned and only came to the club with the purpose of extracting him from the bar. He was good company so that his wife became the club enemy. As soon as she came in sight a warning call went out and Peter was offered his favourite tipple, vodka - in doubles and triples. He would slide round the bar out of the back door, downing his vodka on the way, and just as we were answering his wife's question as to whether we had seen him with a unanimous "No" enter the club behind her and say:

"Hullo Gracie, fancy finding you here."

"Peter Shaw. Where have you been?"

To which he would answer that he had been checking the furniture in a friend's house or sorting out something at the Residency.

"It is time you were home."

"I know, my dear, but as we are at the club how about a drink first. What would you like? I will have a lemonade."

"A triple?" the barman would ask and we rather gave the game away by trying, unsuccessfully, to suppress sniggers.

The Betio club was the opposite in life and character and in no way the stereotyped club of Colonial novels, being neither stuffy nor racially exclusive. The only criterion for membership was to be a lawful drinker and to have the money to pay for your alcohol. Perhaps there was an element of discrimination here for alcohol was forbidden to a native unless he had a permit and a native in terms of the Native Status Ordinance was defined as a "person wholly or partly of Micronesian, Polynesian or Melanesian descent" unless he was domiciled in Fiji.

So, prima facie, a Gilbertese but not an expatriate Fijian, of which there were a number on Betio, had to apply for a permit to drink if he wished to join the club and enjoy its alcoholic facilities. If the District Commissioner and the Island Magistrate of Tarawa agreed you were a responsible person and would not drink a month's salary in two or three nights of binge a permit was not difficult to obtain.

Not so obviously or simply, if a Gilbertese did not wish to obtain a permit but still wished to drink and join the club there was a second course he could

122

take. Under the Native Status Ordinance, as long as he was of "mixed descent", he could ask to be declared a non-native.

Taking this path however, while it eased access to alcohol could severely affect your matrimonial life and your exit therefrom and a careful calculation of advantage and disadvantage had to be made. As a native if your wife laid a charge of adultery against you and you came before the Island Magistrate and his court you could find yourself in gaol for up to seven years. This sentence could be increased if your illicit partner in "carnal knowledge" was a member of your family in the degree of second cousin or closer with the exception that if you were a member of the family of a High Chief, to knock off your second cousin was without penalty. While no such punishment could be applied to non-natives for adultery, divorce for a non-native was a business for the High Court, and intimidatingly expensive. Against this, with native status a divorce could be obtained "if the temperaments of the parties to the marriage are incompatible".

As a non-native could ask to be re-declared a native some richer Gilbertese hopped from one status to another and appeared or disappeared from the club with the ebb and flow of matrimonial fortunes and alcoholic or social needs.

This Betio club was a low cosy building also of Gilbertese materials. It stood near the harbour and the open space behind it which formed the focus of the islet.

Agnes, the barwoman and caretaker, had planted bougainvillea, frangipani and hibiscus round the building. With daily inspection, watering and the application of whatever pig manure Agnes could find they made a broad splash of mauve, cream and red, giving a most attractive approach. The frangipani was continually in flower and its scent blew in through the walls and windows.

Unlike the Bairiki club, which opened for home-going civil servants, the Betio club was accessible the day long. Ships were always coming and going and when they had been at sea for a month or a week captains, mates (if any), chief engineers, assistant engineers (if any) and supercargos would quench thirsts of as long standing as their voyage, for there was no alcohol at sea. Artisans of Fijian descent spent a regular part of each day there and commercial and government staff called after offices shut.

The club was purely social and apart from the bar offered only occasional film shows and a monthly dance or party. A lot of shop was talked and undoubtedly Victoria Bitter and informality helped the smooth execution of the affairs of government and commerce. Business done, expatriates would turn to their own kind, Fijians to Fijians, Australians to Australians and British to British and discuss what was going on or had gone on - sometimes in the distant past - in their home communities. The only broadcasts we could receive clearly were those from the "voice of Hawaii", parochial and often incomprehensible. The only newspapers we had were the weeklies from Britain. By the time they got to us the world and home news was stale and the progress of sporting teams and reviews of theatre, cinema and books were of more interest.

For those who had done Devonshire courses the greatest concern by far was raised by the charts carried by the Times showing the rise and fall of eights in the Oxford and Cambridge river races. Lines leapt and plunged as bumps, over-bumps and double over-bumps were made or lost. An intricate pattern was produced and it required a careful finger to follow criss-crosses showing the progress of boats and the contingent reputation of colleges.

We did have one local broadcast a week. This was from the Government wireless station and after a few items of colony news we tried "20 questions" or similar BBC programmes at which it became my lot to cheer or to bang two bits of wood together to augment the clapping of the studio audience.

At parties we danced to a live band of guitarists. If it was an ordinary party we dressed in open neck white shirts and trousers. If it was an island night we wore the brightest possible shirts - I still have two made from gaudy curtain cloth - and a lavalava, a skirt length of cloth buttoned at the waist. This was normal gear at least for the Europeans and Gilbertese. The Fijians wore much more formal clothes. Usually suits and always ties. One invariably wore a Harris tweed suit with a stiffish collar under his tie. The Harris was of the heaviest and hairiest variety and of a brick-red colour so that when Henry warmed up, which was not very difficult with a starting temperature in the 80s, his face exactly matched the colour of his suit. As the evening went on he became wilder and fiercer, drinking a lot and dancing a jig by himself before the band in the busiest part of the floor, his long black hair falling on to his shoulders and over his face. His wife, who had Indian blood and could have been very dainty, except that Henry had knocked out a number of her teeth, also unfortunately wore too many clothes, having a liking for long flounced dresses, frills and stays. Dancing with her was like taking a moist bolster on to the floor - a similar moist bolster being a visitor from England who was trying to keep her shape with goodness knows what and who, much to our amusement, repeated with horror in her voice that the New Zealander she had partnered had asked her "What do you do for a crust, my beaut?" A question about whose decency she could not be clear.

Unhappily as the evening wore on Henry and his wife inevitably talked about colour. Henry would say he knew he had a black face but his heart was white while his wife spoke with immense pride of one of her children who was much lighter skinned than the others. Sometimes when drunk the part Fijians would fight with each other, not with the Gilbertese or Europeans. The spark igniting their quarrels seemed always to be a racial or sexual slur. If the part Fijians were destructive of each others' persons the Europeans were destructive of property. Scrums were formed against walls which promptly proved they were in need of renovation while rafters sagged from tests of mass and the floor showed holes that indicated they were not Haka proof. There were a few Gilbertese who came to parties and only one ever had anything untoward to say. He had been seconded to the School of Oriental and African Studies teaching a linguist Gilbertese. When maudlin he would complain: "In London which is the headquarters of all the Colonies you can drink all the day and here you can only drink in the evening." That was one unexpected perspective of Empire.

The music to which we danced was very energetic. It had a Pacific stamp to it; not the soft wail that is described as Hawaiian but a thump-thump-thump that was ideal for the "twist" we performed in the days before the western music world invented it. We had for a time American servicemen at a weather station. They thought it wonderful and wriggled, shook and squirmed happily by themselves in corners, eyes glazed but stone cold sober, reminding me of swaying caterpillars I once saw in a tin of bait.

The parties were fun and some incident usually provided gossip for the future. The Met. Officer lost his false teeth outside by the bougainvilleas. He scrambled on all fours in the gloom looking for them, mistook a hermit crab, red body in white shell, for the missing dentures and put it in his mouth where it promptly nipped him. "They don't fit properly" he complained. "They are hurting me".

Women who went to the lavatory found a hand coming through the wall and pinching their bottoms. Reactions varied from giggling to embarrassment and anger. A clique from Bairiki were particularly annoyed and took an oath "never to visit this low Betio club again". Absolution would probably, almost undoubtedly, have been granted by the advent of the next Betio party but there was no need to wait to confirm the degree of their resolution. "Doctor Mac" one of the two doctors on Tarawa and consequently in the Gilberts was at the party and getting exceedingly drunk. He was cautioned that the Loves' baby was due to arrive and that he was expected to attend the birth. His friend Love father was also at the party and Mac went up to him.

"Jimmy there is plenty of time yet is there not?" To which Jimmy replied rather weakly that there was.

"Well there is time for a beer then and one for yourself," and the two Scots set to doing a sword dance with Agnes's brooms crossed on the floor.

A message came that the baby was starting an entry to earthly life and Mac, bottle in hand, was hurried as fast as was possible to a launch accompanied by the male and female white population of Bairiki, some twenty in all. They arrived and, urged on by Jimmy and with a trail of wives in tow, Mac weaved up to the Love house and collapsed on the sand outside the bedroom. Getting his breath he shouted somewhat blurred inquiries into the house, answers came from Jimmy which were repeated in whispers by wives and followed by the shouting of incomprehensible instructions from the man lying on the ground.

It was put to the men by a senior wife that we should go home. "Not a male matter" she said.

The baby arrived safely, Mac and Jimmy had more than one whiskey and the Bairiki wives forgot all about the Betio club.

Unfortunately the nights of parties at the Betio club ended as did my days in the district office and the touring that went with it. I was ordered to transfer with immediate effect to the Secretariat where I was to assume duties as Assistant Secretary (Personnel). So in 24 hours I had packed my belongings, now taking up 3 boxes, handed over my house on the lagoon and reported for duty to my new office.

The Secretariat was head office for the colony. It was of pre-war construction and of entirely Gilbertese materials except for the floor and without a perpendicular or straight wall inside or out. The roof, much re-thatched, sagged, and the exterior bulged and sank and was multi-coloured and striped where it had been patched with new palm ribs or sewn up with new string where the old had frayed.

The interior was gloomy with a grey mould on the walls and exposed timbers soaring to the roof. There were no ceiling and no glass in the square openings which served as windows. Under such a window in the west wall I acquired a desk (where behind my back I could hear the lagoon lapping at high tide), a pile of files, and some advice from the departing incumbent.

"If you get an old file make sure there is not a scorpion in it and keep the whites happy and you will be alright."

If the first piece of advice was practical the second struck me as cynical but proved only too true. There were thirty nine white families on Tarawa and they and their affairs took up far more time (and money) than the affairs of five to six hundred local staff in the colony who, for instance, were philosophically prepared to wait years before the government paid them salary revision arrears, something no white or his wife would have tolerated.

With the Secretary to Government, the civil servant next in importance to the Resident Commissioner and the other assistant secretary I worked long hours, eighty or so a week; Wednesday afternoon (meant to be a holiday), evenings after supper and Saturday mornings. This was not the hardship that it sounds for there were no outside diversions - no cinema, no wireless, no television, no cafe or restaurant and no library. Our only entertainment came at week-ends when there was tennis or sailing in a Gilbertese outrigger, beer in the club and a social life. Not surprisingly the two of us who were unmarried became wedded to our work and even when we had left the office were prepared to talk shop. The policeman who had met me at Ocean Island on arrival in the Colony would have held our life style in very low esteem.

On the outside of our building the only notice was a small piece of varnished wood at the side of one of the two entrances which read "Secretary to Government". This anonymity always struck me as sinister with nothing to indicate that in an unmarked office attached to the main building the Resident Commissioner sat as the man who exercised all effective executive power, the High Commissioner being 1,000 miles to the west, but who rarely signed a letter and, except for heads of departments gatherings over which he presided, exercised his authority largely in personal one on one confidential meetings. It was the Resident Commissioner who could abruptly cut short a career or advance it, reward you with a double increment or withhold your increment, commute a sentence of death, upset or not British-American relations by his part in the administration of the Anglo-American condominium in the Phoenix Islands 1,000 miles east of Tarawa, and approve of the explosion of hydrogen bombs by the Christmas Island base another 1,000 miles east of the Phoenix Islands but still in the Colony.

To little or great extent all civil servants, particularly if they only met the Resident Commissioner at formal dinners or cocktail parties, held in awe the building and its chief occupant, the unnamed and shadowy "Government" who only demonstrated his existence and power by having a Secretary who did his bidding. However, besides the mystery of power the Resident Commissioner also possessed the trappings thereof. Materially he had the only vehicle on the islet, the only launch, both of which flew his flag, a police guard of honour which presided at his going out and coming in by boat and, on the Queen's birthday, impressive splendour; the Royal Standard flew, the police band marched up and down, unfortunate drummer soaked through to his tiger skin (provenance to him completely unknown), and the Resident Commissioner announced from a rostrum the birthday honours starting in my first year in the Secretariat with his own august self: "To be a companion of the Most Distinguished Order of St. Michael and St. George, Marcus Ludovicus Delmonte", and then got on to a series of less meritorious awards.

The Resident Commissioner enjoyed his companionship of this order and certainly regarded it as adding weight to his name to have "CMG" on formal letters and documents before the OBE which he already possessed. However, his solitary eminence in the middling orders of chivalry did not last long. The following year when recommendations for birthday honours were being considered an offer of an MBE was made to the Director of New Construction. This honour, one of the lowest and most routinely awarded, was usually given for long service and good conduct to indigenous (i.e. local) civil servants on retirement, or for twelve or fifteen years service to minor expatriate civil servants, to European women who had shown leadership qualities with girl guides or the like, and to mayors of small towns. The Director of New Construction considered it was not an appropriate award at all. We had a meeting and rather reluctantly it was decided he should be offered an OBE. This he accepted, the High Commissioner agreed and advised the Colonial Office. Surprisingly promptly the Colonial Office replied "Allocation of OBEs for year filled. Director of New Construction Ballenden recommended CBE. Assume no objection."

The Resident Commissioner turned purple when I handed him the encoded telegram but as in his annual confidential reports the Director of New Construction had been given the highest praise he could only mutter "Well, that's that then". But he went home for an early gin and his announcement at the birthday parade of the Director of New Construction's honour "To be a

Commander of the most excellent order of the British Empire Philip Arthur St. John Ballenden" came through teeth half clenched.

The Resident Commissioner's personal staff, i.e. the Secretary to Government and the two assistant secretaries including myself, liked the man we worked for even though we did not agree with the way he ran the Colony at all. He knew what he wanted and worked hard for it, he did not niggle and treated us and his civil service fairly, making us feel what we did was appreciated. We realised that he was self important, sometimes pompous, occasionally highly irritating and that his wife could play too important a part in some of his decisions, but he was human and after he had suffered a heart attack and had to be flown out of the Colony by an urgent flight of the RNZAF from Fiji we dreaded the possibility of having his acting replacement as our permanent superior.

This was a cleverer man, a hard and efficient worker (colonel in the war at 24) who spoke excellent Gilbertese, but had the most appalling manners that we had ever encountered. To cause embarrassment he threw food on the floor at dinner parties, was ostracised by women for referring loudly to his wife's genitalia in the coarsest terms and found fault in the smallest matters of administration in all departments.

Anybody who liked art was "wet" and he boasted of having spent two years at Cambridge without ever entering King's College Chapel. A real mis-fit in a very small colony and an appointment which reflected no credit on the recruitment section of the Colonial Office. When the substantive Resident Commissioner returned Government servants and the public threw him a spontaneous and memorable party.

"Our" Resident Commissioner had a weakness for creating and enjoying excitement. On a minor level he achieved this by hiding classified documents which he found lying where they should not have been. In the evening after hours or early in the morning he would prowl round the Secretariat and hide code books, cypher papers or confidential files in a hole in the floor. When one realised that the papers were missing we grovelled over likely holes feeling under the boards and enlisted the help of our fellow administrators and Sapoa the chief clerk. If we did not find the missing documents a real panic could develop as they might have been gathered up with unclassified material and been filed away anywhere. One way to establish what had happened was to go to the Resident on some pretext and assess his mood. If you were greeted with exceptional goodwill you knew that he had hidden the papers and all was well.

More interestingly and with much less inconvenience to us was the Resident Commissioner's delight in putting the Colony on an emergency footing. This caused us the greatest excitement, particularly as we could not talk freely outside the Secretariat, and made it impossible to do routine work while we played out our part in the emergency or waited on edge and in awe for the Resident Commissioner's moves in the drama.

The United States of America laid claim to parts of the Gilbert and Ellice Islands Colony. The islands claimed included Christmas Island. Before the British had established a base there from which to test nuclear weapons Naval Headquarters in New Zealand reported to the High Commissioner in a routine message that the American 7th Fleet intended to visit it. The High Commissioner was unable to get an answer from the Colonial Office whether the visit had been cleared diplomatically or not and sent a telegram to the Resident Commissioner in which he said "that American forces were attempting an unwarranted infringement of international law and breach of agreed status quo... that Christmas island along with other Line Islands is an integral and important part of Her Majesty's Dominions for which it is my honour and duty to be responsible." He thereupon ended "I authorise and direct you to take all such steps as you consider necessary to support and demonstrate sovereignty."

The Resident Commissioner, whose dislike for his trans-Atlantic cousins was only surpassed in degree by the jealousy with which he regarded his watery domain, more than strongly backed the High Commissioner's view. He had been in the navy and knew exactly what to do before a possible battle. Within 24 hours he had:

a) declared the Gilbert and Ellice Island Colony to be in a state of emergency and ordered all officers to assume duties in accordance with the security plan;

b) organised the censorship of letters and closed wireless stations to private messages;

c) set up a committee to study "the seizure of enemy property" (i.e. the property of American Missionaries);

d) commandeered the Tungaru, the only ship in port (preparing to sail to Suva to have her deck plates replaced), and had her blacked out;

130

e) mobilised the Gilbert and Ellice Islands Armed Constabulary and put forty members of it in an expeditionary force under the command of a District Officer who had been a major in the Parachute Regiment "with powers of detachment commander";

f) issued battle orders to the expeditionary force which included: (i) the need to conserve ammunition "so as to preserve the power to strike effectively"; (ii) the importance of keeping water bottles filled, which were only to be used "if it is necessary to move temporarily to the bush"; and (iii) the taking of salt tablets daily;

g) despatched the expeditionary force under its bemused and somewhat nervous commanding officer at 9 knots to Christmas Island on the Tungaru.

The Resident Commissioner reported to the High Commissioner and was somewhat perturbed to receive a reply that the use of force was to be avoided and that the dangers of over-reaction were to be borne in mind. "Please confirm commander expeditionary force instructed accordingly." This he could not do for contact with Tarawa could not be made with the Tungaru's wireless.

For two weeks the Commanding Officer of the expeditionary force suffered suspense before he found himself in the ward room of an American battleship and something of a hero for having travelled "2000 miles across the Pacific in that banana boat". The Captain of the ship told him the detachment of the Seventh Fleet was visiting the scene of wartime bases and battles. No infringement of British sovereignty or breach of the international status quo was apparently considered. The O.C. Gilbert and Ellice Islands Expeditionary Force thereupon made a very favourable impression upon the American Navy by demonstrating the quantity of gin he could drink while remaining clear headed enough to use the ships wireless to send a message to Tarawa that he had arrived safely and without problems, a message that the Resident Commissioner interpreted as meaning he could also have some appropriate liquid refreshment.

I do not know but doubt whether the Colonial Office heard of this matter.

We had another state of emergency during one of the Middle East crises of the 1950s. This time orders came from London. Leave was cancelled and we were ordered specifically to consider air-raid precautions and the requisition of enemy property. I suspect that the Colonial Office mistakenly relayed Empire-wide telegrams sent to Cyprus, Aden or other middle eastern or Mediterranean territories.

In terms of the security plan for this situation the Senior Auditor was relieved of his auditing duties and became Chief Cypher Officer. The Resident Commissioner on going to the auditor's house to deliver a message for encypherment was enraged to hear the auditor's wife calling out to her husband with much giggling "Immediate" say again "Immediate London British Government with Priority. I have a lovely bunch of coconuts I spell c for Charlie o for orange c for Charlie..." which was as far as she got.

The following week when the Colony had stepped down from its war footing the auditor's wife was most surprised to receive by messenger an envelope with the royal crown on its back. Her surprise turned to suspicion when she opened it and found a card with another coronal embellishment inviting her to morning coffee at the Residency. The messenger had been told to wait for a reply and hurriedly and unhappily she wrote out a pleasurable acceptance and sent it back with him.

A friend inquired on her behalf who else was going to coffee on the day she was invited. All enemies! - and they had been invited personally and not by formal invitation.

The other members of the party were already present when the auditor's wife arrived at the Residency. There was a general scuffle as she came in and she found herself, after being welcomed, in a chair facing a low table. Opposite were the Resident Commissioner's wife and half a dozen of her best friends. These ranged from the wife of the Plumber (Grade II) to the wife of the Accountant General and Collector of Customs (Superscale). They were seated according to the official precedence of their husbands, in diminishing order away from the Resident Commissioner's wife. Coffee was poured out, biscuits offered and some formal and stilted conversation made. The Resident Commissioner's wife put her cup down with a clatter and cleared her throat. All other cups except Mrs Bishop's were put down. The owners assumed expressions between gleeful and pious. The wife of the Resident Commissioner spoke.

"Mrs Bishop. It is very nice to have you here to coffee. We feel we don't really see enough of you. However there is also something we feel it is our duty to speak to you about. We don't of course know your background but, that apart, we feel it is important to keep up standards even though we all know that things are not what they used to be." A sympathetic cluck first made by the Accountant-General's wife ran round the table.

The Resident Commissioner's wife continued. She got round to dress and then foundered. Mrs Bishop was now very red and shaking. She put her cup down, spilling coffee in the saucer.

"I don't see what you mean Mrs Delmonte. Is there something wrong with my clothes?"

The favourite spoke.

"It is your brassiere she means. Why can't you be decent and wear one like the rest of us?"

Mrs Bishop half gasped and half snorted. A glint came into her eye. She looked pointedly at the favourite who was very flat chested.

"You wouldn't know what a brassiere is for. No wonder your husband spends so much time looking at the native girls."

"Ohs", squeaks and one giggle greeted this remark, and tears from the favourite.

Mrs Delmonte spoke.

"I am not accustomed to that sort of talk in my Residency, Mrs Bishop. I would be glad if you would leave us."

Mrs Bishop left, eyes gleaming and cheeks flushed. She walked quickly to the house of the friend who had found out for her who were to be the other guests at the coffee party. The friend was most surprised to see her coming along her path and jumping up and down looking at her heaving blouse as she did so. She went out to meet her. The auditor's wife raised a hot red face.

"I am not indecent Bertha am I?" she demanded.

Bertha who knew the cypher officer story reassured her.

"Of course you are not. But why do you ask?" and when she had heard the put down on the favourite at the coffee party said "It is revenge for the coconuts and you'll not be asked to the Residency again for a long time. I think you did very well. Let's have a drink."

Competing with the excitements of the near states of war into which the colony entered was that created by the High, Resident and District Commissioners and their wives becoming very distressed British subjects. On tour early one morning their ship, Nareau, at full speed hit the island of

Abaiang. By undeserved good luck it ran up a channel in the reef. Damage was light but it was firmly wedged.

The crash was at about 6 a.m. and from then until 8 a.m. when the Betio wireless station opened the Resident Commissioner wrote a series of telegrams in clear directing actions to be taken "with the utmost despatch". This the Secretary to Government, also an ex naval man, explained meant dropping all other work and doing whatever the utmost despatch referred to at top speed. But there was in fact very little that could be done. No Royal Colony Ship was available and we could only charter the Tungaru from the Wholesale Society. This took some time, and many high speed launch trips between Betio and Bairiki, as the Manager of the Society insisted on a written contract. Inquiries about action taken passed hourly between the Secretary to Government and his Government in the shape of the Resident Commissioner on Nareau on Abaiang.

The Resident Commissioner's wife and the District Commissioner later related what was happening on Nareau. Separately they both agreed that the Resident Commissioner put himself in line for another heart attack particularly in view of the, quite innocent, exasperation the High Commissioner's wife caused him.

Lady Lash thought she was on a glorious adventure and wanted to write to her son in England to tell him about her tropical island ship wreck.

She asked "Now this ship is the Nareau isn't it?"

"Yes, Lady Lash."

"And the island's name?"

"Abaiang."

"And where is it on a map? I want to tell Jonathan so he can find it." There was a moment's silence.

The Resident Commissioner spoke and as a former naval officer his words must nearly have choked him as R.N. ships do not go around the world bouncing on or off islands, or not knowing where they are.

"The latitude and longitude is uncertain. I have checked the chart and there is an error."

So Lady Lash muttered "What can I head it?"

Amanda, her daughter, spoke.

"Don't be silly, mummy. Aboard Royal Colony Ship Nareau on a coral reef latitude and longitude uncertain."

"That sounds right dear" and she started her letter.

When she had finished she asked if she could have a swim and the District Commissioner was detailed to escort her. They took the ship's boat and disappeared down the coast.

Fate was not kind to the D.C.. When they got out on a beach there appeared a few yards out the back fin of a shark. Although Lady Lash had spent all of her married life in African colonies before coming to the Pacific she knew what she was looking at.

"Oh dear, there's a shark". Pause. "But he is not going to spoil my swim, are you sharky boy?" and she picked up stones and threw them at the fin. When the fin disappeared she went into the sea and calmly swam out to where it had been. The D.C. joined her but admitted afterwards he was terrified. When he heard about it the Resident Commissioner turned purple. To have lost the High Commissioner's wife as well as a ship in one day would have been an ineradicable blot. As it was, and contrary I suspect to all naval and marine practice, no enquiry in a court or otherwise was ever held into the grounding.

The thought of being a mover or even a power on the world stage obviously appealed to the Resident Commissioner and we suspected he had delusions of Churchillian or Palmerstonian grandeur. However when it came to the exercise of real power and actually pushing or pulling events to happen he was most effective after his lunch time gin. If his landrover came to a skidding halt on the gravel outside the Secretariat we knew there was trouble.

There was a shortage of eggs before an important dinner. The District Commissioner was ordered "forthwith and without fail" to make a collection from villages on Tarawa, the Resident Commissioner launch being put at his disposal.

The Residency oven was not getting hot. An emergency inspection by the Senior Electrician showed that the mains wiring was inadequate. A double wire to the residency was installed within a week while a band of loyal wives agreed not to use their ovens so "poor Kathleen can cook".

The wife of the Residency cook ran away with another man. Devastated, the cook could not perform his duties. The Island Magistrate was ordered to have the offender arrested and tried immediately on a charge of adultery.

Unfortunately the adultery was not that serious in Gilbertese eyes and the cook refused to lay a complaint. Long bouts of eventless office life did not suit the Resident Commissioner. He liked to see things "happening on the ground" and to have control of events, however humble.

Particularly when he had to stay with them on tour, missionaries he found "a dead bore" partially because the non-conformist brand never offered alcohol. He would take his own bottle of gin and spend a long time in the bedroom before the evening meal while his wife ferried in glasses of lime juice.

"Your husband is very thirsty."

"Yes and rather tired, he is lying down for a bit".

When the Resident emerged genial and glowing he usually got "We are glad you are feeling so much better Mr Delmonte".

In the Gilbert islands the prevailing winds were easterly so that western coasts were, for over ninety-nine percent of the times, sheltered. A force ten gale from the west then did enormous damage, blowing down houses and canoe sheds and at the ends of islands where the land was unprotected by a reef hurling up sand and huge blocks of broken coral.

One day we knew in the Secretariat that we were in for a westerly and made sure the blinds over window spaces were tied down and fastened. When the wind started to whistle through the teba of the walls we secured loose papers, took down calendars and notices on partitions and moved our desks into passages, the Resident Commissioner in a high good humour patrolling the building and supervising our work. Then the rain struck, hissing on the outside of the double thickness teba, running down the inside thickness and spraying in a mist where the teba was warped and the wall cracked.

"Protect the files" ordered the Resident and we moved files to sheltered shelving stacking them high. As we were doing this the main hall of the building shuddered and the roof moved an inch or two to the east. We all looked up. The framework of uprights, rafters and beams was in place, and the coir rope and string intact but relationships had changed and there were no even near verticals. As we gazed there was another lurch and a faint sigh audible above the wind.

"I wonder if it will go completely" said the Secretary to Government.

The Resident looked at him.

"Take my landrover and get rope". He said.

"James, go with him to the jail for prisoners and collect some police. Sapoa, we need all clerks to help."

Half an hour later we were all outside in the gale, supervising athletic prisoners and policemen who were climbing up the thatch holding on to ropes thrown over the building and fumbling to pass other ropes through the thatch and around ridge poles. Four ropes attached we heaved on the beach, soaked from rain and sea spray to haul the building back to vertical, exhorted by a dripping Resident Commissioner swearing about knots becoming undone, loud and forceful in his exhortations to pull and in his mind no doubt back in the navy in the days of sail. But despite all his verbal input our efforts were useless and we achieved nothing against the wind.

Fortunately, after an hour or so of give, the building came to an accommodation with the gale and when it had canted twenty degrees and the wind could sweep over it rather than into it, it moved no more. We secured ropes to palms and a pandanus tree and poles as props were placed round the east side of the building.

The Resident Commissioner was a happy man. After organising watches he praised us for our work and disappeared home to write a colourful despatch demanding funds "to rebuild my colony headquarters in a style fitting to its importance and capable of withstanding the forces of nature." Unfortunately his wish was granted and in due course our outwardly charming building disappeared.

10. A MEDICAL EDUCATION

Temporarily I had to leave the Secretariat. This was done with some concern. Firstly I knew that nobody would deal with my work while I was away and that on my return there would be a multi-coloured flood of files round and under my desk with tags "Urgent", "Temporarily Confidential", "Immediate" and on the desk a note listing further files that would be "waiting your attention" in the confidential registry. Secondly, on hearing that I was going into hospital to be treated for amoebic dysentery everybody told me what terrible treatment would be my lot and how feeble I would be when it was finished.

"It's ten days of emetine iodide injections. Peggy had it and she was so weak that she had to have two nurses to hold her up."

"Dick collapsed in the shower from those awful injections. It will be no tennis for three months."

"Your heart can be affected for life. Don't find yourself invalided out."

After the emetine the cure required ten days of retention enemas.

"Cocked upside down for that time" - ribald comment, unprintable - "the amoeba will be annihilated but so will you."

I knew then what to expect. However when the Senior Medical Officer (SMO) said in a hushed voice:

"You will have to go into the maternity ward", it was near panic striking. Anything to do with child birth and babies was completely out of my ken. Only grandmothers, mothers, midwifes and gynaecologists spoke of such matters, and then in hushed tones, giving the whole subject an unpleasant mysteriousness. Talk over-heard of Caesarian births, forceps deliveries, placentas and afterbirths made me squeamish and in my imagination a maternity ward was something approaching a torture chamber with cases of shiny stainless steel instruments, the floor stained and the walls sound-proofed to stifle the cries of the suffering mothers.

It took two hours by launch across the lagoon to the hospital islet and the whole way I turned over in my mind the significance of the maternity ward and wondered what would be in store. When finally I decided that there was something experimental or particularly unpleasant about the treatment coming to me it came as a relief and I relapsed into a state of gloomy anticipation - when you "go over the top" you take what comes but hope for the best.

But all for nothing! The SMO gave me a quick tour of the hospital. There were eighty Gilbertese in two wards, seventy nine with tuberculosis and one with a broken leg, and when he came to a small detached room, neatly thatched, said with smile:

"Not a maternity case but you'll be here. De luxe accommodation by yourself."

When I entered the ward it showed my imagination to have been highly coloured. It was of standard Gilbertese construction exactly like my house and office, rough, dusty and not in the slightest hygienic. Against this, and the only feature that could in any way be rated as "de luxe", was the sight through the window opening of a sparkling blue passage separating the islet from the next, coconut palms leaning over the passage, a bright yellow beach and beyond that the white foam of the surf and an endless blue. Something that I had much missed in the secretariat and a picture which any travel brochure would print. To add to its quality, in the passage, somewhat skew on their stilts, were small thatched platforms with low walls and dipping roofs. Not for mentioning, possibly, in the travel brochure, but public lavatories.

I was left to undress and told to get into bed. A quick look around the ward failed to reveal any stainless steel hidden in cupboards and an opening in a wall led only to a shower. I had a look at the bed. There were no cranks, handles or hinges so it seemed impossible that a body could be enforced to adopt extraordinary postures and below the bottom sheet it showed itself as a usual Gilbertese charpoy, coconut string on a homemade wooden base, the best of beds in a hot climate. Reassured by the surroundings I got into the bed and waited.

While the ward held none of the artefacts of surgery to stimulate nightmares there were other distractions to a calm existence. While I was still allowed to sleep on my back a soft plop awoke me one night. For a few seconds the object that had plopped was still, then it moved and I realised a rat had landed on the bed from the rafters, probably only the small Pacific rat and not a descendant of the European rat that had arrived on Tarawa with the Americans during the war, but certainly a rat and it did not wish to leave the bed. The emetine had worked on my muscles as predicted and I did not feel up to getting out of bed and looking for a weapon to dislodge the rat, nor did

I wish to get bitten or even scratched by trying to hit it with my bare hands. There was no light available but luckily the sheet was well tucked in at the bottom of the bed and I could hold it tightly at the top. When the rat crawled above my stomach I heaved with both hands. The weight in the middle of the sheet disappeared and another soft plop, this time on the floor, told me the rat had left. There was no body in the morning so I assumed he had gone back to the rafters.

A week later, when I was sleeping on my front, there was a much more frightening experience. A clinking noise awoke me and as it got closer I realised it came from chains. Somebody had escaped from the locked compound in which the mad were kept and he was coming towards my ward. I could not run or hide so I froze. The clinking became louder and louder and was added to by a shuffling sound - the chains were round feet. This was a relief as if the mad man or woman did come in to the ward it would probably be possible to get away!

But the noises passed by the door and faded in the direction of the staff houses. I went back to sleep but was awoken again by the same noises, a voice I recognised as one of the doctors, and the flickering of a torch. When they were outside the door I called out. The doctor answered "It is only old Uriam. I am taking him back."

A group of Gilbertese orderlies visited me every evening to give the enema. The first night there was a large crowd and when my pyjamas went down and the enema tube went in there was for a moment a hushed silence. Then somebody said in an awed voice "It is true. He is white all over". I wondered if there had been a bet on it but did not inquire and instead asked my orderlies about Uriam.

"He often gets out and he always goes to Doctor Rees. The doctor has a gift with the i-rangirang (mad). He can make them quiet."

During the day there was almost complete silence. Sometimes the surf could be heard on the reef and sometimes a heron or sea bird. The leprosarium was on the other side of the sea passage outside my window and occasionally there came the voices of lepers raised in argument.

They were an immoral community taken singly when their disease was diagnosed from all islands in the Colony and living outside the social structure of the Gilbertese. For 3 years they took medicine under the supervision of doctors and were well fed with no activity to occupy them except to plot and execute their affairs. Fights were common.

140

I chatted to the two European doctors or matron when they came in briefly to see me and looked forward to my food - thanking God and the medical service that neither I nor Timeon had had any part in preparing it.

However it was all a lull before a storm. In addition to my body being turned upside down my ideas and world view were all about to receive the same treatment - from a stolid Scots doctor, the Senior Medical Officer, who, unlike the majority of administrative officers regarded the Resident Commissioner's foibles and extravagances as other than material for jokes.

He had come from a practice in Cornwall on a three year contract to the colony. Such things as controlling expenditure and preparing estimates had never entered his life and when the forecast he produced for the cost of running his department in the forthcoming financial year showed all his funds being used for the purchase of equipment for an operating theatre that had not been built he had spent many hours in the secretariat sorting out matters with the other assistant secretary and the Accountant General. Staff and running costs were calculated and his new operating theatre became a dream. We had always exchanged talk and he had lunched with me. Now in hospital doing his rounds we spoke a lot of shop. He criticised the expenditure on head-quarters and when I asked him if he had heard that the money refused for a clinic on Bern had gone on a radiogram, decanters and a picnic basket for the Residency he became pale and outspoken.

"There is a drought in the southern Gilberts. Old people and small children, say two to four year olds, are dying. There are no coconuts, so no copra and no money. If you are too old to fish and have no family to support you then you starve and die. If you are a small child and have been weaned, you die of gastro enteritis or malnutrition. The medical department knows this, the district administration knows this and the secretariat knows this. The Resident Commissioner must know this but he turns down a clinic in the middle of the drought islands and buys himself luxuries for his house. I used to believe in the empire but I am now having doubts. I could make a fuss when I get back to England but I doubt if anybody would listen."

I knew that the Resident Commissioner was aware of the situation in the southern Gilberts and said nothing. But I talked nearly daily with the SMO who was not constrained, unlike career administrative officers looking forward to promotions and pensions, in what he said and lent me a book that criticised the administration of a British possession many years previously. The book was titled "Letters of an Indian Judge to an English

141

Gentlewoman" and had been published in New Zealand in the 1920s but unfortunately the name of the publisher and author I have forgotten. The judge who wrote the letters met the woman to whom he wrote when an undergraduate in England before the First World War. They never met again but corresponded for the rest of their lives describing their hopes, fears, marriages and problems at work and in their private lives. The judge criticises the civil service on a number of counts. He recalls the days when justice was done in unpretentious buildings or under trees or in fields at the site of a dispute and regards the construction of large, sometimes vast, courts of law and offices as expensive and unnecessary for the operations of government. He notes the growing conformity among the expatriate civil servants in dress and thought and the increasing weight in the administration given to form rather than action or enterprise. Keeping the British in India were the prospects of advancement in office, honours and, to be enjoyed in a distant homeland, leave and life on pension. For India itself in the most part they cared nothing and often seemed to bear a hatred.

With my India and Far East oriented family the book came as a shock. I did not like it and was not inclined to accept it. Similarly to Winston Churchill when he was told in the 1930s that he should reconsider his views on Indians gleaned from experiences forty years earlier: "I am perfectly satisfied with my views on India and I do not want them changed by any bloody Indian". The SMO and I argued and he tempered my views in part by pointing out that gaining the confidence of a patient was always important. To which I countered: "Yes for a GP but if you are a surgeon or specialist the cure is the thing and you don't have to like your patient" remembering a friend of mine who, as a medical student, had accompanied a surgeon on his rounds and was somewhat shocked to hear him say to a docker on whom he had operated following injury in a particularly violent strike: "Well you are all right but I hope if any of your friends get an injury like that they don't get to hospital on time." However we both agreed that a parallel was to be found in our colony to the maladministration the judge had found in India. Too much money was going on head-quarters (even to my family the building of New Delhi was an expensive nimiety) with an over-use of imported materials making construction costs six times higher than if local materials had been used. Civil servants with a staff of a messenger and typist were being bestowed with titles like "Chief" and "Director" to justify large increases in salary and the enhanced quality of their office space. Even salaries for local staff at headquarters were inflated, some earning ten times as much as an island magistrate, an official far more important to the peace and good administration of the colony than a filing clerk or non-shorthand typist.

But the Resident Commissioner's most serious sin was to give priority to correspondence and business with the Colonial Office regardless of the importance or otherwise of the subject matter. It was clearly his aim to satisfy the wants of London rather than the wants of the colony. The doctor and I agreed this was a disaster.

All expatriate administrators knew the Colonial Office was inefficient. Seconded to that great office of state, they returned to the colonial world with chilling stories of ignorance, cynicism and laziness. There was an anthology of sayings which circulated in colonies concerning this, such as:

"Like the fountains in Trafalgar Square they play from 10 to 4"

(Foreign Office, Victorian).

"Stick close to your desk and never go to sea, and you will be the ruler of the Queen's navy" (HMS Pinafore - inspired by the political career of the original W.H.Smith, of book shop provenance, who soon after entering parliament was appointed First Lord of the Admiralty.)

"The peace of Whitehall which passeth all understanding, preserve your mind in lethargy, your body in inertia and your soul in coma, now and for evermore. Amen" ('Benediction' 1930s Foreign Service).

"The most inefficient office in Whitehall (1950s Colonial Office, Field Marshall Montgomery).

"I have seen a number of shows in London, good, bad and indifferent but the worst was the Colonial Office". (1960s Colonial Governor in Africa).

For the Colonial Office, the divorce from reality was of no concern and there was never, I think, the slightest doubt in the minds of Colonial Office officials of their ability to arrange the government of millions of people thousands of miles from Britain living under desert, jungle, mountainous, oceanic or sub-arctic conditions. Combined with a distrusting attitude towards Governors and all lesser men on the spot there was a belief in the doctrine that what was good for Britain was good for elsewhere and that all colonial subjects were endowed with the wishes, habits and characteristics of British people and merely differed in speech, appearance and superficial religion and customs. There would, in Colonial Office opinion, have been no difficulty in ruling from London a colony of non-hominid star dwellers several light years away from earth, apart from a slightly irritating delay between the despatch of telegrams and the receipt of answers. Suggestions of making visits to Colonies to see conditions at first hand were scorned. "It would prejudice our views" or "We must be detached" were the maxims trotted out in justification of stagnation. The office was a firm believer of the Aristotlean view that it was not necessary to take note of what happened in the world and that all problems could be solved by thought alone.

The capriciousness of Colonial Office rule and ignorance of colonial conditions was a boon to silly or unscrupulous colonial administrators. Any nonsensical or selfish scheme could gain acceptance in London if plausibly presented and accounted. Depending on his integrity and diligence only a colony's auditor could bring to the Colonial Office's notice monstrous examples of tomfoolery or knavery. Even then nobody was likely to be brought to book financially for waste of money or mal-administration. Rather it appeared having made a mark, good or bad, at the Colonial Office an official was recognized as a being of initiative and favoured in promotion over unknown personages.

One example of waste on a serious scale took place at Tarawa over the building of a new Colony headquarters. The pre-World War II headquarters had been on Betio but the treatment it received during the war made it an object of disdain. Over the ocean reef British guns lay battered in the ruins of Japanese emplacements. On the lagoon reef and beaches American landing craft and ships lay rusted and holed. The interior of the islet was hot and windless while the debris of battle, including parts of dead Japanese, could appear anywhere.

Some 20 miles from Betio at the end of the lagoon the Americans had built an air-field on an islet called Bonriki. Here the runway had been preserved and there were workshops and housing.

Government officials can exist in two phases or states. They are either substantive, known often as permanent, or acting. Although they can "act" for a long time, an acting officer only holds office temporarily to keep things going and is not meant to take policy decisions.

In regard to colony headquarters a substantive Resident Commissioner and a substantive High Commissioner agreed that the Colony Headquarters should be re-built on Betio. An acting Resident Commissioner did not like this decision and pushed an acting High Commissioner into agreeing that the Colony Quarters should be on Bonriki to take advantage of the "substantial existing facilities". A rosy report was compiled emphasising the savings in the cost of ship repairs achievable by using these facilities and stating that Bonriki was big enough for the entire Colony headquarters to be built there. The Colonial Office agreed the change in plan without any ado and gave money for building and improvements. Workshops were built or refurbished for ship repairs, the air field tidied up, a base built for flying boats, accommodation provided and staff moved. Then the test day arrived. A missionary ship in need of repairs was offered the use of the new facilities. But the captain refused to go. The Tarawa lagoon was, he said, not only shallow and beset with coral nigger-heads but was uncharted. He would not hazard his ship. The acting Resident Commissioner blustered and bullied but to no avail. He spoke to two government captains who looked for a channel, found none and said they supported the missionary captain. A Gilbertese clerk was called in. What had the Americans done in the war with Bonriki? Had they used it for ships or not? Not at all for ships, said the clerk, only by sea for launches. Ships had used Betio. I do not know what story was given to the Colonial Office but the next Resident Commissioner started to move the Colony Headquarters back to Betio and Bairiki. When I was in the Colony there were at Bonriki only the airfield flying boat facilities and a rusting heap of British money.

So we lived in an empire that was decaying and smallest wheel that I was in the Colonial Service machine the bickering, suspicion, corruption, double standards and indecisiveness that occur in failing institutions were very obvious and became accepted in our lives. To make sense of their work Colonial Servants could only "bash on regardless" while counting up the compensation for loss of office that was increasing monthly by their remaining at their desks. There was one matter, however, which did shock the near dead body of the Colonial Office to life. A parliamentary question, trivial or serious produced a spasm of action and put off the hour of rigor mortis.

11. A PARLIAMENTARY QUESTION

In the south of the Ellice Islands, some 900 miles from Tarawa, is the island of Niulakita. It is small, wet, and fertile. As landing can be difficult and on account of its remoteness it is only rarely seen by officials. However it was fortuitously visited by a Mrs St John Beckett, the wife of a Member of Parliament who was on a ship doing rounds of mission stations in the south Pacific and loading copra where it could.

The good lady went ashore to escape smells and to have a walk. The Captain of the ship gave her as an escort and interpreter an Ellice deck-hand who spoke English.

At first she looked round the little village near the landing area and spoke to one or two people. She thought the small open-sided houses were charming while the colourfully dressed men and women talked to her politely and without reserve. Coconut palms rustled overhead and after the vibration and noise of the ship the quiet dusty road with a few scratching chickens and the murmur of waves on the reef was restful and soothing.

With her interpreter and half a dozen children trailing behind she walked along a path that meandered away from the village into the coconut groves. She had not gone very far when she heard a noise like a moo. She stopped abruptly.

"What is that?" she asked.

The interpreter struggled with his English.

"It is not quite a cow, madam, but it has four legs."

"Whose is it?"

The interpreter spoke to the children.

"They say it is nobody's, madam, it is uncultivated."

"Uncultivated?"

"Yes, madam. It runs around and nobody looks after it,"

"You mean wild, my man."

"Wild, yes, wild madam."

The woman paused for a moment.

"I think then we had better go back to the village."

"That would be as well, madam. The children say the animal has spines on its head like a sword fish which it might stick into people."

"Spines? You mean horns. Of course it has. All animals like cows have horns. Has anybody been hurt by it?"

The interpreter spoke again to the children.

"Yes, somebody has been kicked by it."

"Are the children frightened of it?"

None of the children answered the interpreter when he spoke. He questioned them again. A small girl answered.

"Yes, I am frightened. I do not like to go near them and one ate the copra my brother was making and he had to run away."

"Madam, they are frightened of them and they chase away people who like to make copra."

"What has the Government done about it?"

"The children say the policeman who came to the island two years ago was told of it but nothing has happened."

"It is too bad the things that go on in these out of the way places. It is slack officialdom and I will have something done about it." She went back to the ship.

The Captain was supervising the loading of the copra. Mrs St John Beckett spoke to him.

"It is too disgraceful that in this day and age such conditions should exist under the Union Jack. The poor islanders are terrified to go out of the village. Some wild sort of cattle are rampaging in the countryside and they can't even make copra."

"Bison I expect" said the Captain.

"Yes, very probably bison. I want to send a telegram to the Resident Commissioner immediately. I shall certainly tell my husband of this most unhappy situation."

The Resident Commissioner who received the telegram was only temporarily in office, the substantive Resident Commissioner being on leave. Before joining the Colonial Government he had been a Major in the Indian Army and during his career in the Gilbert and Ellice Islands he had performed some matters of note. He had suggested, for instance, to the captain of a ship that he move his plimsoll line when the captain complained that his ship was "down to the line" and it prevented him from loading any more cargo; he had added two species to the list of protected birds much to the satisfaction of the High Commissioner, who was a keen ornithologist; and he had rowed himself out in a skiff to disarm a ship's engineer who had gone mad and who had driven everybody off his boat by shooting at them with a rifle.

When he had read the telegram he minuted:

a) that the animals would probably be buffaloes rather than bison.

b) that the Secretary to Government was to find out if Mrs St John Beckett or her family had not been in Bangalore.

c) that the District Commissioner should take a gun on his next tour to the Ellice Islands and shoot off the buffaloes if they were in fact proving troublesome.

d) that the hole in the paper through which the file lace passed had been punched 3/4" instead of 1" from the edge contrary to standing order.

A month later a telegram arrived from the Colonial Office asking for information on the wild bison "assumed to be bos bubatis bubatis" terrorising an island believed to be called Niulakita and adversely affecting economic activity, particularly agriculture, on the island.

The Colonial Office asked for an assurance that the island existed and was a British possession as there was no indication of it on their map.

A reply was urgently requested so that an answer to a possible parliamentary question could be prepared.

The Acting Resident Commissioner replied that the District Commissioner would visit Niulakita in the course of his next administrative tour to the Ellice Islands but would only shoot the animals if he in fact found them to be troublesome. He suggested that the animals were probably buffalo not bison and confirmed that Niulakita was indeed under British rule.

In their reply, the Colonial Office said that as Mrs Beckett (wife of Mr Humphrey Beckett M.P.) had reported the bison to be troublesome to the local population they should officially be so considered. It was asked that the District Commissioner's tour be expedited and suggested that consideration be given to other methods of destroying the animals than by shooting. Until such time as positive identification was possible they should be referred to as buffalo/bison to indicate that their status was uncertain.

Major Murphy was not sure what to do about this telegram. He appreciated he was not a "good office wallah" so he consulted the Secretary to Government, who knew exactly what to do and sent a reply saying that due to lack of funds the District Commissioner had curtailed his touring programme and could not visit Niulakita until the next financial year. Thereafter the Colonial Office was silent.

The Resident Commissioner returned from leave and the quiet life we had enjoyed under the supervision of Major James Murphy, D.S.O. late Assamese Horse, came to an end. His Honour pounded around our offices demanding information about what had happened during his absence and rang the filing clerk's bell every few minutes. A number of the files he inspected landed on my desk including one named "General - Fauna and Flora - 1 General". On it, I knew, following a pamphlet badly chewed by fish moths on methods of exterminating rhinoceros beetle, was Mrs Beckett's telegram from Niulakita and the telegrams exchanged with the Colonial Office. I opened it with interest. On a large sheet of clean white paper in a large hand His Honour had written:

"I fail to see why such important matters are not pursued with more diligence and prosecution during my absence from my Colony."

A fulsome letter to Mrs Beckett followed recording the Government's appreciation of her services to the Colony and inviting her to stay on her next visit at the Residency "where I can assure you there are no disagreeable wild beasts".

This was followed by a minute to myself telling me to draft an urgent telegram to the Colonial Office asking for funds so that the District Commissioner could "undertake the soonest possible visit to Niulakita". This I did and then went to see my colleague, the other assistant secretary. We gossiped and when I mentioned the Niulakita matter he said:

"Murphy would never have done that but Monte smells a chance of promotion". I agreed.

There was silence on the matter for a month and then we got a coded telegram.

"Urgent. B.G. with priority."

"Secret and Guard Addressed Hicom Honiara repeated Rescom Tarawa. Wild buffalo stroke Bison Niulakita. In view of political importance of matter and likelihood of questions House of Commons Williams Head of Pacific and Antarctic Dependencies department wishes to visit Niulakita and establish personally situation with regard to wild buffalo stroke bison."

More followed and the telegram ended: "Please confirm urgently island exists. Location here not proved possible."

Plans were made and funds obtained from London with a rapidity which was unbelievable. The District Commissioner Gilbert and Ellice Islands District was given overall command of the expedition to Niulakita and as a start decided that the shooting party would need training additional to that offered by the Gilbert and Ellice Islands armed constabulary. As the officially appointed trainer, but never having shot anything larger than a rabbit in my life, I turned to Mrs Murphy for help.

While Major Murphy had shot a lot in India he had turned to conservation and birding in middle age. Not so his wife. In her house she kept a '22 always in reach and an eye on the thatch roof. If she saw a rat on rafter or beam her gun was up, visitors fell silent and there was a bang followed by a grunting "got him" (always male!) and the descent of furry body to floor or furniture. A loud "Onions" and her house-boy would pad in to remove the corpse.

"Ever done any buffalo shootin'?" she asked me.

"No" I said, so Mrs Murphy lent me a book "Some Animals I Have Shot" by a Colonel Fox-Gower, with a picture on the front cover of a fierce looking man in puttees and solar helmet astride a rhinoceros.

"Poor old Fanny" she said "Dead now but knew his stuff. Read the chapter on buffalo."

I did that, and then got further personal instruction from Mrs Murphy.

"Only shot of any use with a buffalo is a heart shot. If he charges, puts his head down and top of his skull, you've got the horns. No use trying to get through that. Certainly not with those peashooter 303s you've got. Aim for the heart. Front or side - any idea where it is? No? We'll need a dummy. Mark it out."

A brisk inter-departmental correspondence followed before a coconut leaf and sacking buffalo was made by the Department of New Construction and suspended on a pulley and line by the Mechanical Engineer. Mrs Murphy objected to the absence of a tail.

"Swats and swishes, and you'll find it distracting through the sights."

The Department of New Construction said they would be happy to add a tail but making it "swish and swat" was the responsibility of the Department of the Mechanical Engineer. The Mechanical Engineer said he had no funds with which to buy the equipment to make the tail of a fabricated buffalo/bison swish and swat in a realistic fashion. Mrs Murphy insisted it was necessary upon which the Mechanical Engineer referred the matter to the Auditor. The Auditor said the expenditure could not be approved without getting the views of the Director General of Colonial Audit, particularly as the necessary mechanisms would have to be made in Melbourne "which would seem unduly expensive" and that there was no head of expenditure to which this cost could be charged.

So we had a buffalo/bison with an immobile tail but with a red heart which was shot at front and side by a team of five constables and a corporal. The training finished, and the expedition equipped, it disappeared from our secretariat lives and we awaited further news with some anticipation.

12. SAVING THE NIULAKITANS

Colonial Governors lived in very splendid style. If their colony dated from the 18th century such as in the West Indies their house was the size of a large country house of that time. In the 19th and 20th centuries the size remained large while the style changed to that of the massive imperial produced by Sir Herbert Baker. These houses were furnished free, stocked with duty free liquor, maintained free and supplied with free ornamental policemen as the governor saw fit. Large and attractive gardens surrounded Government House and large and well polished motors were available to take the governor, his family and guests where they willed. A governor had royal status, was entitled to a royal bow, was commander in chief of any armed forces in his domain and could if he wished over-rule legislative and executive councils and legislate by decree. All in all a very splendid personage and commonly considered in the Colonial Service as the nearest approach to God on the surface of the globe. KCMG was a common honour for governors and it was with a ring of truth that this was translated as "Kindly call me God" (The grandest governors were given GCMG, said to stand for "God calls me God"). But all governors stood on pedestals if not of clay at least movable and removable by far lesser beings, unknown and unremovable. Beings who were not well paid, who were perkless, who commuted in crowded trains, who were garden-less, servant-less, weighed by debt to building societies and who spent their working hours in bare cold offices in central London. Such a being was George Hercules Williams, the head of the Pacific Department of the Colonial Office, grey with a straggly wet moustache above which he continually sniffed, reminding people of a rabbit in a field undecided whether to eat more grass or not, and known to the clerical staff as "bunny". The grandee enjoying gubernatorial status for whose doings he was responsible was His Excellency Sir Frederick Murchison, Her Britannic Majesty's High Commissioner for the Western Pacific. Sir Frederick received the news of Williams' visit with a grunt. He realised he would have to accompany him to Niulakita to ensure that there was not undue interference - spelling in his view "trouble" - in the affairs of a territory under his rule. There was an exchange of many "telegram-savings" between Honiara and Tarawa and much input from the High Commissioner's daughter Ursula, who as an economy measure he had appointed his ADC thereby saving the allowance he would have been expected to make out of his own pocket to an ADC on secondment from one of the armed services.

Plans were made and re-made but finally a date for the visit was set and communicated to the Magistrate and Island Council of Niulakita.

For the people of Niulakita the news of the visit generated immense excitement and they staged a memorable and comprehensive welcome for the officials. Nobody on the island had ever met the Resident Commissioner and the High Commissioner, superior to the Resident and who lived thousands of miles away across the ocean, was a complete mystery in appearance and in habit.

The Resident, although not known in the flesh had a baggage of gossip attached to his person which was transported from island to island and ship to ship by islanders who even at third or further removed hand had seen him in person or heard him described in habit and appearance. In particular his custom when staying overnight with abstemious missionaries of having copious supplies of lime juice sent to his bedroom before dinner was well known and the subject of speculation, as was his fleshy face for going dark red under stress, his silver grey hair and heavy spectacles. But the High Commissioner was a mystery. Even the Queen far far away to whom he reported and who was their ultimate ruler was better known. There were official photographs in all government offices of Her Majesty and there were people who had heard her speak at Christmas over the wireless. But the man whose name was only known on paper from regulations he had approved or laws (beginning "Whereas it is expedient") that he had signed and enacted, and who in so doing regulated their lives was unknown, completely and utterly.

So in ignorance but in awe of the great man's coming the Niulakitans worked for days to greet him and show their appreciation of his visit. In monetary terms, as they had next to no money, the costs of the welcome were non-existent but in terms of labour, mental and physical, involved in planning the provision of food and presents, the costs were vast.

On the day on which the new wireless station told them the High and Resident Commissioners, their wives and daughter as well as the District Commissioner and an important man from the Queen's office for all the colonies in London were due to arrive a grandson of the magistrate's was sent up a coconut palm at daybreak to report when the ship was in sight. In the middle of the morning be called "Sail-O Sail-O". Word was passed round the island and laughing, calling and giggling the entire population, in their smartest clothes, grass or cotton, moved to the landing area. The island's canoes put to sea, the paddlers shiny with oil and when the ship arrived, reversed and stopped engines and drifted to a halt they paddled to form a wide slowly moving circle round it, all eyes turning to the back deck. There, a group of three European men and three European women returned the gaze of the Polynesians. The men except for swords and medal ribbons were in white from shoes to helmets, their ladies in floral frocks, wide brimmed hats and long gloves. Not on deck was Williams. When he had left London, the Permanent Secretary had said "Well enjoy your visit to the south seas." Very decidedly he had not done that.

Rather he had found it all hellish. He had never travelled by plane and discovered that he disliked flying. America was strange, noisy and unintelligible. Canton Island where the plane had refuelled was the end of the earth but an end with a beach on which he had become in ten minutes burnt and blistered. In Fiji he lost his way in the spaces of Government House seeking a lavatory and at a cocktail party, the only man not in a dinner jacket, he was the target of a monologue by a chief 6 foot 6, very black who leaned over him and expatiated on the evils of the Indians in Fiji. Australia he also did not take to, was as near to being astounded as he could be at the amount of meat eaten at breakfast by large sun-tanned men in his hotel, and learnt that he was a pom and as such not a member of a respected tribe. Honiara was sticky and hot and at Government House for some social peccadillo he realised he had committed but could not identify, he was excluded by Ursula from the after dinner carpet bowls. On the boat he decided spending the day in his bunk, even with the pervasive smell of diesel, was the best place to be, well away from the others and their talk of fishing, sport, unknown native tribes in unknown parts of the world, and references sly and not so sly to the evils and inefficiencies of Whitehall. He had thought with longing of suburbia, his house and partly finished rug and had wondered what awfulness Niulakita would bring. Unexpectedly, it brought him early in the morning one joy, a nearly still boat.

He had ten minutes of peace and rest broken by the falsely solicitous voice of Ursula. "Time to get up, Mr Williams. Ready for breakfast are you? It's on the back deck and then you will have to change for going ashore".

His traveling companions were enjoying watching the encircling canoes when a loud groan and a muffled croak of "help" came from the companion way leading to their deck. With a groan of rather different timbre the High Commissioner said "Williams" and Ursula loudly "I will see to it" and went to the companionway and looked down.

In the opening a skin of white foam palpitating like milk about to boil rose and sunk and Ursula shouted "Are you in there Mr. Williams?"

"It is me, no, no it is I, and I am caught in my mosquito net. I need urgent help please, very urgent help."

"There is no need to bring your net on deck. The cabin steward will air it".

"No, no Miss Murchison, it is not my bed net. It's part of my helmet for protection ashore. It seems to be caught, firmly caught and I cannot move, no, not in the slightest".

"I see what it is. You are hitched on a screw. I can soon get you off that."

She knelt and fiddled.

"Got it. Now you can come," and the foam rose, showed itself as net, and spilled on to the deck supported by its inner content of man who put out two leather gloved hands to grasp a rail. In the space from a ring which supported it some inches from the man's helmet to where it was tucked in at his waist, the foam was dry and ruffled in the slight breeze that blew across the deck but from a piece of felt at the back of the man's neck to shirt cuffs, waist and knees, the cloth was sodden and adherent to flesh.

"Hm" said the High Commissioner, reflected, said "hmmm" again and then "spine pad there I see. No need for a spine pad, went out with the ark." Overcome with his loquacity he went silent, staring ferociously.

Ursula backed him.

"H.E. is quite right and you will not need all that other gear. What are those gloves for?"

"Not gloves Miss Murchison, gauntlets".

"Well yes I see. But what do you need them for?"

Williams looked astonished. "Against snakes. Butchers (outfitters in London) assured me that extreme precautions were needed."

An argument or, perhaps a heated discussion took place with Williams championing Butchers as the infallible authority on tropical dress, saying he would feel much more self assured following their expert advice.

"But my husband's colony has no snakes, Mr Williams, except two legged ones that walk by night" Mrs Delmonte snickered.

155

"No snakes, Mrs Delmonte, no snakes? But Butchers said throughout the tropics snakes, venomous snakes, snakes even of the extremest toxicity were common. Arboreal where there is suitable flora. Terrestrial where the habitat is unfavourable to arboreal species. Universally found they said, and in some areas where there are spitting species it is even wise to wear special glasses".

Ursula had been looking determined since Mrs Delmonte had referred to "My husband's colony" and now got her oar in. "This colony of my father's is quite free of snakes, Mr Williams. You need have no fears at all. And you don't need that mosquito netting during the day."

Williams regarded her with disbelief and muttered on about Butchers in London, seemingly regarding both location and shop as infallible and beyond reproach.

Ursula's face showed a flicker of contempt but she continued in as soothing a tone as she could manage.

"But Mr Williams, we must look after you carefully, you realise, and if we capsize when we go ashore it will be very difficult for you to swim in those clothes."

"Capsize! Capsize into the sea? Is that possible? No, not possible. I realise it must be possible, but probable?"

Williams looked towards the beach and paled.

"Poor swimmer. I am a poor swimmer, Miss Murchison, and will certainly change. But sharks, are there not sharks here? To undergo the risk of capsizing would seem hazardous and unwarranted. I have no insurance, none at all" and he went off to his cabin muttering that he should have been provided by Butchers with shark repellent.

The District Commissioner signalled a canoe and when it had tied up alongside the ship reported to the Resident Commissioner that it was ready to take him ashore. "Yes time to go Mr. Delmonte" said Ursula. The Resident looked over the side.

"Where is my flag?" creating a bout of unsuccessful scuffling and searching.

Eventually the High Commissioner said "Short trip, Delmonte, go without it."

"He can't do that, Daddy" said Ursula. "He must fly his flag and you must fly yours. Otherwise it won't be clear who is coming."

Eventually the flag was found and the Resident's party went ashore where the flag was rushed to its pole and raised.

The canoe returned to the ship and the High Commissioner and his party boarded. Ursula gave the High Commissioner's flag to the bow man in the canoe who tied it to a spar. They paddled to the beach, where eight Ellice Islanders were waiting with chairs. The Europeans sat, were lifted and unsteadily carried up the slope, Ursula shouting "Bring the flag, bring the flag."

They were deposited at the top of the sand, in front of them were the Resident and District Commissioners, a guard of honour and in three sides of a square the entire population of Niulakita.

"Royal salute. Present arms" shouted the sergeant of the guard. The Gilbert and Ellice Islands Colony armed constabulary came to the present, two bugles blew and a drum rattled.

The Resident Commissioner marched up to the High Commissioner and saluted, and the High Commissioner returned the salute. They then shook hands, the Resident slightly dipping his head and saying; "Welcome to Your Excellency's Colony of the Gilbert and Ellice Islands, Sir" to which he got a grunted reply which may have been "Hm, very glad to he here". As these words were reluctantly extruded the High Commissioner's flag was run up and formally the ruler of Niulakita had landed, the leader of a force which would impress upon the Niulakitans that the predation of the formidable buffalo/bison upon their way of life would be ended.

Quite what Williams had expected about the modus operandi of the extermination expedition is not known. Perhaps he thought there would be the establishment of an office to which reports would be made and where he would sit or maybe that he would accompany the field force and witness the destruction of the prey or, more to his liking, he would make an inspection of the dead and receive a reliably certified report that there had been total destruction of the unwanted beasts. What he certainly had not expected was the lengthy welcome given by the many groups who wished to show their pleasure at the High Commissioner's visit. He was looking around for somewhere to shelter when Ursula ordered:

"Mr. Williams you will please follow H.E., Mr Delmonte and the D.C. and it would be best if you took that handkerchief off your head and did not salute bare headed. You have duties you know. Come on now" and he was marched off to shake hands with the members of the Island Council.

It turned out to be the worst, if most educative, day of Williams' life. The gory banner depicting Christ with an exposed red dripping heart and tubes round which members of the Sacred Heart Mission gathered to sing Ave Maria made him feel squeamish, the theme song of the Seventh Day Adventists primary school, "Temperance Boys and Girls are we" caused him to ask the District Commissioner whether there was a drinking problem on the island, and the answer that nobody on the island drank at all left him confused. Finally when the choir of the London Missionary Society ended God Save the Queen at the third verse, wishing confusion and frustration on the Queen's enemies he was nearly beside himself and muttered aloud about the United Nations not liking such thoughts, that they were completely out of place in the modern world and he would send out a circular when back in London. Soto voce Ursula said it was splendid and the Resident Commissioner, rather more explicitly, that having had the entire able-bodied male population of the island carried off by South American slave traders in the 19th century, a seizure never repeated after Queen Victoria declared a protectorate over the islands in 1893, and having suffered rapes by Japanese soldiers in the 20th century, nobody on the island would wish the Queen's enemies well and as for the modern world they probably did not mind if they were in it or not. The sight of a bloated filarial leg and a half noseless ex-leper in the island hospital brought home to Williams that indeed he was not entirely in the modern world and he could only comment "Interesting" in the compound of the jail where an elderly inmate had been incarcerated for urinating within five fathoms of his neighbour's hut.

The D.C. explained: "Did it deliberately so that he had to come here. His family has to feed him and the magistrate says he hopes they won't, as he wants an acceptable reason to disinherit them." However when they moved into the large and only cell of the jail and saw three young boys well below imprisonment age sound asleep he could not contain himself and came out with "Oh my God." The High Commissioner's face turned mauve and he thundered out "Explanation Delmonte". Delmonte turned to the D.C. "Explanation Bass". Bass turned to the sergeant warder "Explanation Kalifi" and Kalifi turned to the junior warder "Explanation Sapoa". Ursula broke in "H.E. needs a full account. Don't try to hide anything my man. You will be dealt with most severely", and the junior warder ran to fetch the wireless operator.

"Terrible, terrible," said Williams "Bos bubatis bubatis terrorising the population and now under-age children in jail. What would parliament say?

What if Mr. Brockway or Mrs. Castle got to know? Resignation of the minister. Fall of the government. This must be kept confidential, completely confidential, even a secret. Yes secret. It could do the utmost harm."

The wireless operator arrived. "Those are the children that sniffed my petrol. They were drunk and noisy and then they fell down and slept. I called the police and they said they should not be around with the important people coming to the island so we put them in here".

"Quite right too" said Ursula.

The sergeant warder added; "As soon as they wake and we can find their parents they will be let out".

"Quite right too" repeated Ursula. The High Commissioner grunted, the Resident and District Commissioners said "Good" and Williams "Yes, yes. I am sure that is best but nobody is to hear anything about it" and they went off on the path across the island to the rest-house with an escort of police.

Williams looked around the building and said it did not seem very safe with open spaces in the walls and doors which did not shut properly and had no locks. Ursula said it was perfectly safe. H.E. and her mother had often slept in such houses and they were much better than a cabin on a ship. Williams thought for a moment. "Yes, certainly better than a cabin Miss Murchison. Could I try it here please? I am such a poor sailor".

"Daddy will certainly approve of that", to which Daddy grunted "and I am sure Mr. Bass can make arrangements".

"Certainly, Miss Murchison. Mr. Williams can have the sleep-out" and he indicated a small cabin under the nearest palms.

In the evening in the rest-house Williams asked the D.C. what there would be to eat at the feast they were to attend that night. The D.C. advised him that in the food set before them there would be pork, better avoided, several sorts of fish, octopus, crayfish and shellfish, adding that the cooking might not be of the best.

"Yes, Mr. Bass, I quite understand. It will be difficult without electricity or gas but we could always send it back if it is under-done. Octopus and crayfish you say and tuna I suppose? Delightful, delightful. I shall be strengthened for the fray tomorrow and may pick up some ideas for a nice little restaurant I know in Penge. Ha ha. Fish is one of my favourites".

The anticipation of the feast was the end of Williams' pleasures for the evening. In the maneaba it was agony upon agony. Sitting on the floor cross legged, which he had not done since childhood, was near paralysing and he extended and retracted his legs without finding comfort in any position. He made a particular effort during the speeches of welcome when the party was told at length of the appreciation their visit gave to the people of Niulakita and the interest shown in the affairs of the island; however he made a loud groan at quite the wrong moment and was embarrassed when the island dresser came to him and asked if he was ill. A band started, playing the regimental march of the United States Marine Corps on two guitars and a stringed broom handle held on a box as the continuo. Seven girls with flowers in their hair and circlets of flowers in their hands lined up with backs to the band. A whistle blew and slowly, grass skirts swaying and arms gesturing right and left, they shuffled in small steps towards the seated officials and their wives and daughter, the scent of frangipani and oil preceding them. The whistle blew again "Bow your head" said Bass to Williams. He did so as if for the execution block, felt something damp, looked up and saw like the others that he had received nothing more lethal than a circlet of frangipani flowers. The girls stepped back, the whistle blew and they turned round and left the floor, breathing hard and trying not to giggle.

There was singing and more dancing and then, on another blast of the commanding whistle, food, steaming or cold on "plates" of banana leaves was laid before all in the maneaba. Each European and the older men acquired a girl who sat on the opposite side of his piled up meal and fanned away flies. Songs ended and graces were said, three denominations contributing three different prayers after a secular introduction by the magistrate. There was a pause and silence and a very old man started to get up.

Unhappily Williams had been eyeing the food in front of him. "Mr. Bass" he whispered "Do we get knives and forks or chopsticks?"

"No. Fingers only.."

"It is a substantial, most substantial meal Mr. Bass. How much are we supposed to eat?"

"Ssh" said Ursula but they ignored her.

"A piece of everything at least. Your girl is watching".

160

"Ah so. Quite, quite".

The old man had got upright and was holding a piece of fish on high. He brought it down and with a loud smacking of lips bit it. A sigh ran through the maneaba and everybody started to eat.

Williams took hold of a fish and gouged a section out of its middle. A length of intestine was included and as the surrounding flesh parted hanging on the gut appeared three thin white tubes, the longest perhaps five inches.

"Worms Mr. Williams. They have been well cooked so there is no danger in eating them. If you don't want to, the flesh near the backbone is usually free but to show you enjoy the food you should eat the head. Both the Gilbertese and Ellice consider it the best part of the fish".

Williams said nothing but went rather pale. He put down the fish in his hand and turned the body so he could no longer see the parasites then dug a finger in, took a small piece out of the back and with closed eyes swallowed it. The rest of the meal gave him as little or less pleasure. The shark was coarse, the octopus tentacles tough with the suckers coming off when chewed and remaining between his teeth in hard rubbery pieces and a length of sand worm requiring minutes of masticating to reduce it to a swallowable state.

Ursula said "What fun? And to think Americans in Fiji pay anything for a feast and a tame one at that".

The islanders ate as if the meal had to last them weeks. The Europeans destroyed sufficient fish and sticky pudding to make the resultant debris look as if they had eaten enough for politeness sake.

A bowl of water was passed round and Williams took the opportunity to take out and clean his false teeth, much to the interest of his fly girl and the girls sitting to the left and right.

"Mr. Bass" he said, I need to use a lavatory. "Taken short as they say, taken short. Can somebody conduct me to the nearest?"

"Mr Williams, the nearest lavatory, indeed the only lavatory, is in the rest house."

"Across the island?"

"Yes, across the island."

"Is there not a public lavatory here, surely there must be one?"

"No Mr. Williams. We asked for money from the Colonial Office but it was turned down. Savings had to be found we were told."

He looked most embarrassed. "It was the Treasury, Mr. Bass, the Treasury, not us. I will make a special case, no special representations in London."

"Mr. Williams do you want to pass water or is it the other?"

"Both, Mr. Bass, both I am sorry to say."

So the D.C. told him to go out and along the beach and use it below high water mark, "I will get my clerk to guide you. If you like he will find a pandanis leaf so that you can clean yourself but make sure you pull it in the right direction, it has prickles along the edges and if you pull in the wrong direction there can be a very sore cut. Otherwise you can wash in the sea."

"Should I take a police guard with me, Mr. Bass?"

The D.C. said this was not necessary and sent him off with a clerk.

He came back in a quarter of an hour or so and with great difficulty and with a deep sigh squatted on his mat. There was a break in the dancing as the Gilbertese who had come with the party wanted to dance for the Ellice. They assembled at the end of the building and then the crowd behind them made way and on to the floor stepped male Gilbertese and two girls, naked except for flowers in their hair and short fringes of palm strips across their crotches.

The dancing started and Williams viewed it with horror.

The men were in a vee formation, narrow end farthest from the guests, with the girls in line between the men at the ends of the arms. Slowly and deliberately they stepped towards the Europeans.

Besides Williams, other members of the party were also embarrassed by the advancing naked females. The High and Resident Commissioners stared at photographs of King George VI and his Queen on a rafter (royalty only obtaining a view of the girls from the rear) but every now and again when the girls moved forward a step or changed a movement of their arms, eyes would flick down. Lady Murchison was entranced, Mrs. Belmonte half smiled and half leered and Ursula was furious and also looked at the royal pictures but for shorter periods than her father. The District Commissioner was comparing the girls with others he had seen, in between keeping an eye on Williams - who was turning alternately pink and pale, squirming on his mat and trying to look anywhere but at the advancing girls, their shapely breasts with purple aureoles and glistening oil, their narrow waists and flat bellies and

162

the hint of pubescent darkness at the crotch beneath the fringe of leaves. He tried royalty but not successfully and he tried the male dancers but they wore mats which folded into ugly creases so that their body movements were not attractive and their dancing and arm movements were in any case all directed towards the girls. He rather lost his head and at one stage asked the District Commissioner in a loud whisper "We won't have to dance with them will we Mr. Bass?"

Reluctantly, the D.C. had to say no.

The evening ended. The High Commissioner made a speech of thanks. Presents were left and the Europeans exited the maneaba and assembled at the landing station. The District Commissioner had had a good evening and he now wondered if there was further entertainment in store.

He knew that the High Commissioner when in uniform liked to stand to attention in the boat bringing him to his ship when leaving an island and return the salute of those saluting him from the shore. As an aid to stability a junior officer in the boat or, in the absence of a suitable man, Ursula was required to kneel and hold his ankles. Once on a much talked of occasion Lady Murchison had to do the holding, her dress was caught on the propeller shaft and instantly but painlessly removed. The montage of the departing imperial power was broken and the High Commissioner had to give her his uniform coat for cover. A second performance, the District Commissioner hoped, would be well worth the viewing and offered potential gossip value. However, there was no saluting.

"See you tomorrow Mr. Bass" from Ursula signifying the end of proceedings and he and Williams went to the rest house - Williams to the sleep-out, Bass to the bedroom.

Bass was awakened by a howl followed by a crash and the splintering of wood. Jumping out of bed he grabbed his torch and opened the door. He shone the light round the living room and saw Williams in striped pyjamas leaning against a roof post. He was standing on one foot and rubbing the toes of the other foot with his hand. Beside him the low wall which surrounded the room was smashed. The bar running along the top had broken in the middle and pieces of snapped wood tied with string stuck out at all angles.

"Mr. Bass. Do something with them. Do something with them. Send them away. Send them away."

Bass looked puzzled. He noticed William's very red face.

163

"Mosquitoes, Mr. Williams. Have you a hole in your net?"

"No no, Mr. Bass. Not mosquitoes, not mosquitoes, it is these women, these women who keep bothering me. I can't sleep at all - I recognize one of them. She was the girl in front of me at that ghastly meal. White dress with a sash. She comes to the door and giggles; giggles for a few minutes and then goes away and another comes. Giggling, going and coming, giggling, going and coming all the night."

"But, Mr. Williams, she spent the evening keeping flies off your food. That must, I think, be considered a personal service. You have your obligations."

"Obligations, Mr Bass, what obligations?"

The District Commissioner went to a table and ruffled some papers. He produced a book and shone the torch on its cover.

"Instructions and Hints for Touring Officers."

Opening the book he read further,

"This amended edition approved by the Secretary of State in his telegram-saving F7/539/P.A.C./P.233/C. of 7th August 1948. Confidential."

"Confidential, Mr Bass. Confidential, let us lower our voices, lower our voices."

"Here, section 7, paragraph e of the Ellice section,"

"Yes, Mr. Bass. Yes Mr, Bass. I cannot recall it."

Bass read "Officers touring in the Ellice Islands must appreciate that in common with other Polynesian peoples Ellice views on matters of sexual relationships are considerably different to those generally accepted in Britain." Bass paused then continued "In particular it is considered the height of rudeness to refuse the advances of a member of the opposite sex who has rendered one a personal service. While officers then, it is appreciated, may hold their own views on sexual matters, they should, as far as possible, without forcing themselves to violate strongly held principles, conform with local custom. (NB Venereal disease is almost unknown in the Ellice Islands but should it be contracted or any suspicious symptoms manifest themselves after a visit to the islands, the Senior Medical Officer at Tarawa should be referred to at the earliest convenience)."

"Oh, Mr Bass. Oh, Oh.. "

"Well I'm afraid there it is Mr. Williams. Confidential telegram-saving F7/539/P.A.C./P.233/C. of 7th August 1948."

When he was awakened by the wireless operator next morning the District Commissioner sluiced himself. Dried and dressed he went to William's sleep-out and knocked on the door. There was no answer and he looked inside. There was no trace of Williams. He sent a policeman to look far him and in the middle of breakfast he arrived.

"Slept on the beach, slept on the beach, Mr. Bass. Most unpleasant experience, most unpleasant." With his face unshaven and swollen from the bites of mosquitoes and sand-flies he looked indeed as if he had suffered.

"Let me advise you Mr. Williams, have a wash and a change and then go to the Nareau before it leaves for the south of the Island. You can have a sleep and then watch the hunt."

"Yes, yes, sleep! Think I will. Most thoughtful of you, Mr. Bass, most thoughtful." He paused and the District Commissioner said "Is there anything else Mr. Williams?"

Williams reddened and his moustache did its bunny twitch. "Yes Mr. Bass, yes. That leaf I had to use last night, you remember Mr. Bass?"

"Yes indeed on the beach".

"I did not take care, no not sufficient care despite your excellent, most excellent advice. It cut me and now I am most sore".

The D.C. thought.

"Mr. Williams it must be disinfected. I have very little but if you let me put it on it will be enough."

"Certainly Mr. Bass certainly", and the sharp intake of breath when the iodine was applied brought a very tight smile to the D.C.'s face.

Williams went back to the ship and the District Commissioner went to the south of the island with policemen armed with 303s. He picked an open area which could be seen from the Nareau and from which any buffalo/bison leaving the bush would give a clear target. Two shots were fired to tell the beaters they could start. For an hour and a half nothing happened then a faint noise was heard which grew into a minor cacophony of shouts, whistles and the beating of pots and pans. The policemen knelt and rifles were loaded and cocked. Suddenly an animal crashed out of the bush about sixty yards away.

The D.C. ordered the corporal on the right of the line of police to shoot. The excited man responded energetically, swung his rifle so that the stock hit his neighbour on the head and pulled the trigger while doing so, sending a bullet over the palms in the general direction of the west coast of north America. The struck constable collapsed in a heap and the buffalo/bison started to gallop. Taking no chances the D.C. ordered the remaining four constables "rapid fire" and the animal fell, was visited and found to be dead.

The squad returned to their positions and the unconscious man recovered, no worse for his enforced sleep but looking rather sheepish. The beaters were coming closer and a volunteer was called to take a message to the magistrate. The first man to put up his hand was the constable who had been knocked out. The other policemen laughed long and loud. "He did not see the beast. He does not know their speed."

"He was asleep for the hunt."

"He was resting while we were working and now he is strong."

"Tell the magistrate we have killed one" said the D.C. "find out how far away he is and how many animals they have seen."

The constable picked up a bicycle and disappeared down the road.

Suddenly the corporal shouted "Look here comes the messenger and there is an animal behind him." Indeed it was so. The messenger was pedalling as fast as he could and a buffalo/bison was behind him, head down and going about the same speed. There was no possibility of getting a shot as they were in line and coming straight for the party. The D.C. ordered "Run to the beach and take cover behind the bank at the top."

The messenger was almost up to the guns and thinking he would find safety with them turned off the road. The bicycle promptly skidded in the sand, the messenger came off and rolled into the middle of the shooting party. There was chaos and seeing a beater in the distance the D.C. shouted "Nobody shoot." Head down the buffalo/bison came panting past, continuing on the road. Not to take chances the D.C. decided on a volley.

"Pick up rifles, ready, aim, fire." But every shot missed. Leaves fell off a palm, herons flew out of others but the animal galloped on, only stopping when it came to the end of the land and the start of the Pacific Ocean. A second volley felled it.

In the court house that afternoon, without the sleeping Williams, there was a discussion proceeding on colony affairs with the Island Council when the wireless operator arrived. "Your Excellency. Your Honour Your Worship. Excuse me please but here is an immediate from Tarawa in code."

"I'll take it" said Ursula and the Resident said to the High Commissioner who was looking at a picture of King George VI in naval uniform at the end of the court house and getting visibly angry "Your Excellency, this may be important. Can we adjourn the meeting on your behalf while we decode?"

"That picture of the King has been sent all over the world. Seven single gold rings is no known naval rank. Meant to be Admiral of the Fleet of course. Bloody Colonial Office. think they would get something like that right. Yes adjourn."

The officials went to the Magistrate's office. Ursula produced a code book and got to work with the District Commissioner. The telegram read:

"5th December Personal for Williams GTC stop parliamentary question set down wild buffalo stroke bison of Niulakita stop records indicate figures eight repeat eight crossbred Fijian cattle imported Niulakita figures one nine three eight to establish beef industry with view to export and strengthening and diversification of colony economy secers dispatch figures fifty seven stroke eighty three repeat figures fifty seven stroke eighty three of twenty five September one nine three nine refers stop grateful earliest telegraphic report success of industry stimulation given economy and relationship bos bubatis bubatis domestic cattle. Earliest reply required by secer ends secgov".

The Resident said "I must say this development is somewhat unexpected. I will refer the matter to H.E. - H.E. would you look at this please" and he gave the High Commissioner the telegram to read.

The High Commissioner glared at it.

"Hm-hm. Pencil."

He wrote on a piece of paper and then handed it to the Resident and District Commissioners, with Ursula peering over their shoulders. They all looked at one another then encoded the following:

Immediate Secgov Tarawa 6th. December. GTC Immediate Secer London. Yrtel 5th. December wild buffaloes/bison Niulakita. Regret Williams incapacitated and unable to reply. However confirm repeat confirm only wild bovines existing on island. Owing exigencies war and shortage of funds supervision imported Fijian crossbred cattle not repeat not possible and strong indications reverted to type. Buffalo stroke bison presently exterminated unmanageable and in course of extermination operations personnel narrowly escaped substantial personal injury.

New paragraph two. Extermination great relief people of island and fuller lives with increased economic activity expected to result.

New paragraph three. Grateful convey warmest thanks self Rescom colony island of Niulakita to Mrs. Beckett for original information.

New paragraph four Full written dispatch follows. Ends.

So was information provided to answer a question in the Mother of Parliaments, and Ursula for once voiced all our thoughts:

"Well done Daddy."

THE END

POST SCRIPT

After six years in the South Pacific, my father's next posting was to Swaziland, the closest British territory to South Africa, the home country of my mother, whom he had met on a skiing holiday in Austria, and married in England in 1962. He served there from 1962 until 1970 (two years after independence) before returning to England and switching from the (rapidly diminishing) colonial service to the home civil service. In 1972, he was seconded to be part of the UK government's royal commission of inquiry, headed by Lord Pearce, into the Rhodesian regime's proposals for the limited enfranchisement of Africans. The commission's verdict was an unqualified rejection of these proposals. Eventually, the "grey commuter life" in London proved too much for him and in 1974 we emigrated to South Africa, where he became the master in charge of outward bound at Woodridge College, a boys' school in the Eastern Cape that was modelled on Gordonstoun in Scotland, where he also taught history and maths. After this, in a final change of career, he set up and managed, together with my mother, a successful physiotherapy business in Port Elizabeth, while also playing an active role as a volunteer with the Eastern Cape branch of the Wildlife Society. In 2007, my parents retired to Hoekwil, a small village near the coastal city of George in the Western Cape, where my father died suddenly on 21 December 2013, aged 84, leaving behind his wife, Marion, three children (all born in Swaziland), and eight grandchildren.

Proof

Made in the USA
Charleston, SC
29 September 2014